PLAIN ENGLISH AT WORK

Plain English at Work

A Guide to Writing and Speaking

EDWARD P. BAILEY, JR.

New York   Oxford
OXFORD UNIVERSITY PRESS
1996

Oxford University Press

Oxford   New York

Athens Auckland Bangkok Bombay
Calcutta Cape Town Dar es Salaam Delhi
Florence Hong Kong Istanbul Karachi
Kuala Lumpur Madras Madrid Melbourne
Mexico City Nairobi Paris Singapore
Taipei Tokyo Toronto

and associated companies in
Berlin Ibadan

Published by Oxford University Press, Inc.,
198 Madison Avenue, New York, New York 10016

Oxford is a registered trademark of Oxford University Press

Library of Congress Cataloging-in-Publication Data
Bailey, Edward P.
Plain English at work: a guide to writing and speaking
Edward P. Bailey, Jr.
p. cm.
Combines and updates the author's earlier works: The plain English approach to business
writing and A practical guide for business speaking.
Includes index
ISBN 0-19-510449-8
1. English language—Business English. 2. Business presentations.
3. Business communication. 4. Business writing. I. Title.
PE1115.B245 1996
808'.06665—dc20   95-43712

1 3 5 7 9 8 6 4 2

Printed in the United States of America
on acid-free paper

For my wife, Janet,

and daughters, Laura and Jeannette

Introduction

This book combines—and significantly updates—two previously separate books of mine:

- *The Plain English Approach to Business Writing*
- *A Practical Guide for Business Speaking*

The goal of both books was similar: to help people communicate clearly and easily to busy people at work.

Plain English is the key. It helps you as a writer *and* as a speaker. Combining the previous books now gives you help in two very important types of communication for people in business: writing and speaking.

Here's what I suggest:

- If you think your more immediate need has to do with writing, just read the chapters in order. The writing part begins the book.

- If, however, your more immediate need is to give a good presentation, turn to Chapter 17 and start there.

If you decide to start with Chapter 17, though, I urge you to return eventually to the beginning of the book and read the part on writing. The writing and speaking parts of the book complement and reinforce each other.

You should find plain English a very practical, effective, and easy way to communicate. For me, and for many others, it has been a real breakthrough, a lifting of a burden.

✣   ✣   ✣

I continue to express my gratitude to two people who helped lead me to plain English many years ago. One I never met: Rudolf Flesch. But I read his books and found them wonderfully motivating. The other person, Dr. Tom Murawski, is one of my best friends. He gave me one of those books by Flesch and has inspired me ever since.

Other people have been very helpful:

- Janet Hiller, my wife, who read and commented on everything. She is terrific.

- Brooke Bailey (my brother) and Cathy Bailey (his wife) for their excellent advice on the draft of this book.

- Sister P. J. Cahill and Professors Joan Feeney, Charles Hurst, Arthur Meiners, Robert Sigethy, and Maribeth Wyvill—my colleagues at Marymount University.

- Dr. Jim Gaston—friend and colleague for nearly 20 years.

- Dr. Terry Bangs—a consummate speaker.

- Don Insko, who made important contributions to the graphical elements of this book.

- Dr. Fred Kiley, Dr. Greg Foster, Dr. Joe Goldberg, and Ms. Judy Clark—my friends at the National Defense University.

- Reviewers Max Boot, Bob Brofft, Jim Casimir.

- Marilou and Edward Bailey, my parents; and Jeannette and Laura, my daughters. They provided inspiration.

My thanks to my students—both at Marymount University and in classes I have taught to my business clients—who contributed excellent examples of plain English for this book: Dr. Robert Anthony, Sharon Breighner, Alison Furlough, Michael Gallagher, Serge Illaryonov, Jeffery Jenkins, Brenda Jones, Michael Kopito, Sheila Marion, Doyle Mitchell, John Motz, Pennye Perez, Angelica Rayhrer, Danielle Rice, Guy Sahatjian, Susan Shelton, Deborah Tompkins, Brenda Wagner, Antoinette Washington, and David Witmer.

My acknowledgment to the Coca-Cola Company for granting me permission to use its trademark.

Finally, my appreciation to those at Oxford University Press: Liz Maguire (my editor), Joellyn Ausanka, and Elda Rotor. I am indeed fortunate to have worked with Oxford and with them.

Fairfax Station, Virginia   E . P. B.
January 1996

Contents

SPEAKING CLEARLY & EASILY

WRITING
CLEARLY
&
EASILY

THE NEW WAY
TO WRITE

CHAPTER 1

What is plain English writing?

Bottom line

Plain English writing is easier to read—and easier to write. It can express the range of ideas, from simple to complex.

When I first came across plain English, I was teaching writing in college. You can guess what I had been teaching: an overly formal style designed more to impress than simply to communicate clearly to the reader.

Since then, I've switched to plain English and taught it extensively—in college and to many thousands of people in government and business. This book is a result of those experiences, and it's designed to help you discover plain English.

When you make that discovery, you will find that writing is much easier for you—and it will be better, too.

What is plain English?

Plain English, to put it simply, is a way of expressing your ideas clearly in writing and speaking. As for plain English writing, I think of it as having three parts:

- *Style.* By style, I mean how to write clear, readable sentences. My advice is simple: write more the way you talk. This may sound simple, but it's a powerful metaphor that can revolutionize your writing.

- *Organization.* I suggest starting with your main point almost all the time. That doesn't mean it has to be your first sentence (though it can be)—just that it should come early and be extremely easy to find.

- *Layout.* This is the appearance of the page and your words on it. Headings, bullets, and other techniques of white space help your reader see—visually—the underlying structure of your writing. The value is immense. I think of layout as fun to do, and easy, too, with today's computers.

Plain English is not limited to expressing only simple ideas: it works for all kinds of writing—from an internal memo to a complicated technical report. It can handle any level of complexity.

What *isn't* plain English writing?

Businessese isn't plain English, nor is academese, bureaucratese, legalese, or any other "-ese."

Here's an example of some businessese from a federal regulation:

> Each application shall be supported by a comprehensive letter of explanation in duplicate. This letter shall set forth all the facts required to present to this office a complete disclosure of the transaction.

Those of you with business experience know this example is just beginning businessese, relatively uncomplicated compared with what the true Masters of Gobbledygook can turn out.

Nevertheless, it could be more straightforward. Here's a better version. Notice that it loses no preciseness:

You must send us the following:

- one copy of your application
- two copies of a letter explaining the complete details of your transaction

See the difference? You can understand the first version with a little effort, but you'd hate to read several paragraphs—or pages—in that style. The second version won't win the Nobel Prize for literature, but it *is* straightforward communication.

And, at times, plain English does approach art. A clean, straightforward document can be beautiful in its simplicity and efficiency.

Why is plain English better than the "other way"?

Plain English has two important advantages over the other way of writing:

- It's far easier for your reader to read.
- It's far easier for you to write.

You don't need many more advantages than those, do you? But let's look further.

In the past, plain English seemed merely a preference: you like the old way; I like plain English. Who's to decide? Well, psycholinguists have simplified the decision. Their work shows clearly that plain English is easier for all of us to read, no matter how smart we are. And no matter how much experience we have as readers.

For example, psycholinguists have learned that we all take longer to read less familiar words (like *commence*) than familiar ones (like *begin*). The difference is only a few hundred milliseconds in time—but a lot less strain on the short-term memory (and the older I get, the less strain I want to put on mine).

The implication? As writers, we can help our readers by preferring ordinary words.

That's just one very brief example of what the psycholinguists have been up to. I investigate their work at length in another book, *Writing Clearly: A Contemporary Approach.*

Because of the work of psycholinguists, writing style is no longer like the width of lapels: "What's the style this year—wide or narrow?" Instead, there's solid scientific underpinning for the plain English movement.

There's a further reason for writing plain English, too.

Suppose you're the boss—a manager with 15 people working for you. A prestigious project comes in, requiring a report. Only two of your people are both qualified to work on it and have time available:

- One has a straightforward style that's easy for you and your client to understand.

- The other laboriously churns out complex, bureaucratic products that make you reach for the aspirin bottle.

Who will you choose?

If you assign the project to the bad writer, you know you'll have to do extensive rewriting (and maybe most of the writing, too). On the other hand, if you assign the project to the good writer, you can do what you're paid to do: manage. And the final product will be much better because you can spend your time evaluating drafts for content instead of struggling simply to decipher them.

Who is writing plain English these days?

It's hard to believe, but many people still write businessese. But many have also shifted to plain English. In other words, there's a "fence"—with some people on the bureaucratic side and others on the plain English side.

Fortunately, more and more people are moving to the plain English side—and when people reach that side, they never jump back. The advantages of plain English are just too obvious.

Also, many large organizations today are endorsing plain English:

- *Private business.* Many successful companies require plain English. Major improvement in writing has occurred in the fields of insurance, computers, banking, and health care.

- *Federal agencies.* Many (perhaps *most*) federal agencies are training their people to write in plain English.

- *U.S. military.* Each military service strongly urges plain English—by regulation (and those regulations are in plain English, too).

- *Scientific and engineering organizations.* Many of these organizations have to be able to express their ideas to lay people.

- *And even lawyers!* Too many lawyers still depend on the language of the Magna Charta, but even this "iceberg" is starting to slide into the sea. There are, for example, sample wills and other standard documents available to lawyers in plain English.

The move today is clearly toward plain English because it works. It can work for you, too. This book will show you how to write it.

What's the structure
of this part of the book?

The next three chapters introduce the three fundamentals of writing in plain English: style, organization, and layout. The rest of this part of the book then goes into more detail on each of the fundamentals.

For example, after you get the fundamentals of layout in Chapter 4, later chapters will cover other topics of layout such as choosing typefaces, designing effective headings, and using graphics. There are chapters expanding on style and organization, too.

❖   ❖   ❖

So let's begin the journey. For many, it has changed their lives. I know it has changed mine.

CHAPTER 2

Style: writing a readable sentence

Bottom line

Write more the way you talk—with ordinary words, a variety of punctuation, personal pronouns, and contractions.

Let's start with a quiz. Choose "a" or "b":

How have you produced most of the words in your life?
a. by writing them
b. by speaking them

For most of us, the answer is "b": we've *spoken* many more words than we've written.

"What does that have to do with writing?" you may ask.

Everything. You see, in plain English, words and sentences are more like those in spoken English. Spoken English is the language we're most comfortable with—the language that works for us.

That's why most professional writers use spoken English when they write. Check the editorial section of your newspaper. What do you find there?

If your paper is typical, you'll find the editors use spoken English. Look in one of the most popular papers in the world: the *Wall Street Journal.* You'll certainly find spoken English there.

In fact, the biggest headline on page one of every *Wall Street Journal* is "What's News—." The contraction makes the tone informal, and the dash leads the reader into the text that follows. Informal tone and awareness of the reader are two common characteristics of plain English.

The key advice: "Write the way you talk"

Thus, the key to plain English is this: talk to your reader. Simply talk on paper. Write the way you talk.

Imagine you're actually standing in front of your reader. Or talking on the telephone. What would you say—in an organized and polite way? Then write those words.

Sound simplistic? Some people are afraid that "writing the way you talk" means being simple-minded, writing like a kindergartner. But that would be true only if you talk like a kindergartner. The advice is to write the way *you* talk. Look for spoken English: look in magazines, newspapers, successful books. And *listen* for it, too: listen to the most moving speeches, the best newscasts.

What you will find is that the best of writing and the best of speaking have much in common. And what they have in common produces plain English.

Should we *really* write the way we talk?

Well . . . we don't want to write the way we sometimes talk, complete with the occasional "uhs" and rambling, disconnected sentences.

But if you imagine a reader in front of you, if you imagine you are actually talking on paper to that reader, the words will come out like the best of speaking—and the best of writing, too.

Tip
_____

> *For the next thing you write, try putting down the words as you would actually say them. That's what I do: I sit in front of a computer, "talking" through the keyboard to my imaginary reader.*

_____

Don't worry about the theoretical differences between writing and speaking. Simply talk on paper.

Specific tips for writing the way you talk

To talk on paper, you may have to change your writing. For example, when you write:

- Do you normally use words like *commence* instead of *begin,* and *prior to* instead of *before?*

- Do you normally avoid all marks of punctuation except the period and the comma?

- Do you normally avoid using any personal pronouns—like *I, we,* and *you?*

If so, you're a typical bureaucratic writer. Get ready to take the most important step in your writing career. Here's what I suggest:

- Use ordinary words.

- Use a variety of punctuation.

- Use more personal pronouns.

- Use contractions.

If you're like me before I began writing plain English, these suggestions may seem like heresy, like crimes against the English language. Now, though, I think I committed my crimes before I followed these suggestions—not after.

Let's examine those four suggestions in more detail.

Use ordinary words

Which column do you normally choose your words from when you're writing?

advise	tell
assist	help
commence	begin
furnish	give
prior to	before

If you're the way I used to be, you probably choose from the left-hand side.

In fact, when I first saw a list like this, I was shocked to find that I chose *most* of my words from the left-hand side. And I could have given you very good reasons, too—something to do with nuances of meaning.

Then I noticed that when I spoke I consistently used words from the *right-hand* side. Why were the nuances so important when I wrote but not when I talked?

After serious soul-searching, I realized that the so-called nuances weren't really there at all. Instead, I had come to believe that I needed to write with a formal tone—that was the real reason I was choosing the more "impressive" words. As a result, I'd stopped writing with my most important vocabulary: the words I use in speaking each day.

So here's my advice on words. Do as the good professionals do:

- Good professionals use *ordinary* words unless they need something more precise—which happens fairly often.

- But bad amateurs use *impressive* words all the time— unless they can't think of them.

To see what I mean, let's look at writing by a successful professional, Russell Baker. This is the first paragraph of one of his books, *Growing Up* (which won the Pulitzer Prize). He's telling us about his mother, who's in a nursing home but doesn't realize she's there. She's living in the past.

As you read, notice that the passage says *extraordinary* things with *ordinary* words:

> At the age of eighty my mother had her last bad fall, and after that her mind wandered free through time. Some days she went to weddings and funerals that had taken place half a century earlier. On others she presided over family dinners cooked on Sunday afternoons for children who were now gray with age. Through all this, she lay in bed but moved across time, traveling among the dead decades with a speed and an ease beyond the gift of physical science.

Absolutely terrific, isn't it? And where are the "impressive" words? About the only one is *presided*—a good choice that gives us the sense of the matriarch, the woman in control. As I said, such choices help with preciseness.

But ordinary words are precise, too. Do any of Baker's phrases stand out as especially nice? I like "her mind wandered free through time." Where's the "impressive" word there? There isn't one—yet the idea is far from ordinary or simple. And preciseness? The word *wandered*—a perfectly plain word—is right on target.

Writing with ordinary words doesn't mean writing with kindergarten language or producing only simple-minded ideas.

Writing with "impressive" words does mean making the reader's job harder. Even though we know all the words in the left-hand column, we have more trouble reading them, particularly if many appear in the same sentence or paragraph. And they usually do if writers consistently choose their words from the left-hand side.

For example, let's look at a sentence with mainly impressive words:

> Subsequent to the passage of subject legislation, it is incumbent upon you to advise your organization to comply with it.

And if we rewrite that sentence with ordinary words:

> After the law passes, you must tell your people to comply with it.

Would you rather read pages of the first version or the second?

By the way, the second version keeps the phrase "comply with it." It could have said something like "follow it," but the word *comply* seems to make the message a little more urgent. So I don't suggest you always choose the ordinary word. But—to use a word from computer terminology—make ordinary words your *default*. Choose other words if preciseness demands, just as you do when you speak.

And ask yourself what words Russell Baker (the professional who wrote about his mother) would choose if he were writing your document.

For a list of simpler words and phrases, see Appendix A.

Use a variety of punctuation

The second suggestion on style is to use a variety of punctuation. Too often business writers use only periods and commas.

Have you ever heard anybody speak in a monotone? Well, people who write with only periods and commas are like speakers who speak in a monotone, forcing you—the audience—to do too much work: "What was important in that sentence? What's going to be carried over to the next sentence?" The audience has to figure that out because the speaker, using a monotone, isn't helping.

Good speakers do help, though. They use hand gestures and voice inflection to help their listeners along. Good writers, using spoken English, allow punctuation to replace those hand gestures and that voice inflection.

This chapter doesn't cover all the important marks of punctuation you need to learn. A later chapter does that. But this chapter does look at one easy punctuation mark— the question mark—to illustrate the need for more than periods and commas.

A number of years ago, someone asked if I ever used questions in my writing. I realized that I never did, and I didn't know why. So let me ask you now: "Do you use questions in your writing? If you look at the last ten pages you've written, will you find any?"

If your answer is "yes," you know one of the secrets of effective writing. If your answer is "no," that means you're generating your sentences very differently when you write and when you talk—undoubtedly, you use questions often in your talking. And the sentence structure in good talking is better than the sentence structure in typical bureaucratic writing.

So let's look more closely at when to use questions in writing. One time is when you really have a question:

- When does the new copying machine get here?
- How far is Santa Fe from Albuquerque?

Too often, though, people "write around" the question: "Request this office be informed of when the copying machine will be delivered." The shift away from the question is a shift toward writing in a monotone. Your question—often the very purpose for writing—loses emphasis, doesn't it? So don't avoid the question mark when you're asking for something. The reader will more likely take notice of the question because of the emphasis it receives.

Now let's focus on another time to use the question: the question that you, the writer, will answer. Such questions focus what you're saying and emphasize your answer—just as vocal inflection and hand gestures do when you're talking. In other words, such questions draw the reader in.

Let's look at an example. Here's some writing in a monotone (without questions):

> The main point is that the defective computer disks are not the responsibility of the manufacturer, as we first suspected, but of the wholesaler, who stored them at a 130 degree temperature.

Now let's add questions:

> Just who's responsible for the defective computer disks? Is it the manufacturer, as we first suspected? No. The *wholesaler* is responsible—he stored them at a 130 degree temperature.

See the difference questions make? I know. I cheated. In addition to the question mark, I also used a really short sentence ("No."), italics, and a dash.

You don't need to use these techniques in every line you write. But if you're not using them at all, then you're probably communicating with far less emphasis in writing than in speaking.

So the message is to use a variety of punctuation to control your emphasis and replace the hand gestures and voice inflection we all use in speaking. The question mark is one easy way to start. Chapter 8 tells you about other important marks.

Use more personal pronouns

Now for an even more important question: "Do you ever use personal pronouns in your writing?" In some audiences I speak to, about half the people say yes. In others, almost everyone uses them. In still other audiences, almost no one. Yet the value of using them is immense.

In fact, I've never worked with an organization that avoided pronouns and wrote clearly.

Here are the important pronouns for plain English:

First person: *I, me, my, mine, we, us, our, ours*

Second person: *you, your, yours*

Many of us learned at some time not to use these personal pronouns. That idea comes partly from the outdated notion that important business writing must be formal.

Yet the notion of what makes good writing is changing, and a more personal, informal tone is gaining wide acceptance for all kinds of writing.

Another reason people write without personal pronouns is to seem more objective—as though removing pronouns (especially first person) somehow removes all human fallibility. I remember asking one of the top executives in a federal agency what he felt about his people using first person pronouns.

The conversation went like this:

Me: "Some of your people feel they shouldn't use first person—*I, me, we*—in their writing because they'd seem to be giving their opinions. What do you think?"

> Him: "I *hire* people for their opinions! Personal pronouns
>   are an *excellent* way for them to express their
>   opinions—to me and to anyone else."

Don't bosses often hire people for the judgment they can exercise—in other words, for their opinions?

Not too long ago, some organizations even objected to the second person pronoun, *you.* For example, can you imagine reading a book telling how to do something if the book never used the pronoun *you?* The early computer manuals did just that:

> The monitor must first be turned on and then the com-
> puter must be turned on. A menu with the . . .

The computer industry learned that manuals need to be user friendly. And user friendly means talking on paper to the users. Now you're more likely to find a computer manual saying this:

> First, turn on the monitor. Then turn on the computer.
> You'll then see a menu with . . .

The differences in these two short samples are few, but users of entire computer manuals certainly noted the change in approach (and so did the writers of those manuals and the sellers of computers and computer products!).

One reason for using pronouns is that you will more likely use active—instead of passive—voice. The passage from the old-style computer manual, for example, uses passive voice for both verbs.

Chapter 6 discusses passive voice in detail, but you've certainly heard of its bad reputation. Passive sentences are usually harder to read, especially if the content is complex or if several of them appear in a row. So one reason to use personal pronouns is that your sentences will more likely be in active voice and, thus, easier to read.

Another reason to use pronouns is that you can *write* more easily with them. Can you imagine talking without ever using personal pronouns? I try that experiment during my classes, giving a volunteer a topic and then asking the volunteer to tell us about it without using *I, me, you,* and so forth. The volunteer immediately becomes uncomfortable, stays silent a few seconds, and then begins with something like this: "Uh."

Without exception, the volunteers say that trying to talk without personal pronouns is extremely difficult. They also report that when they do find words to speak, those words usually express different ideas—not quite what the volunteers wanted to say in the first place but only what they could say.

In other words, not only was communication harder, but the content changed to meet the artificial requirement of not using the pronouns.

In business, how often do you want your people to alter their content to meet the same artificial requirement?

When we try to write without using personal pronouns—as many people do—we have to put a "mental editor" between our thoughts and the page (or computer screen). That mental editor tries desperately to strip out personal pronouns and restate the ideas without them. Writing with that mental editor is hard work. And, as most professional writers have discovered, it's unnecessary, too.

So the next time you write, talk on paper, and let the personal pronouns come naturally.

Must you always use pronouns to be a good writer? No. Some writing—just like some speaking—simply doesn't call for them. For example, if you're describing a disk drive (instead of telling how to use it), you probably won't need personal pronouns at all: "A disk drive has three major components: the housing mechanism, the drive head, and the . . .").

The key, then, isn't really to use personal pronouns: the key is to stop avoiding them. You don't try to *use* pronouns when you're talking, but you certainly don't try to *avoid* them, either, do you? Just use the same system for your writing.

So get rid of that tyrannical mental editor. And start "*un*avoiding" a few pronouns!

Use contractions

What about contractions? Will using words like *can't* and *we'll* really help your writing? In the past, I pushed contractions only very gently. This time, I'm going to give a stronger message: Yes!! Contractions can make a significant difference in your writing.

You're *much* more likely to write plain English if you use contractions. In fact, it's hard to use a contraction in a sentence and have anything else in the sentence be bureaucratic.

That is, if you're in the mode of using contractions, you're also in the mode of using ordinary words, pronouns, and the entire arsenal that makes up plain English.

In fact, if you're a boss, try encouraging your people to use contractions freely. You'll be surprised how much else in their writing changes for the better.

A concern people have is that the tone of their writing will be too chatty if they're using contractions. I don't think so. We read contractions in professional writing all the time without feeling that the tone is chatty.

For example, look at the *Wall Street Journal.* You'll see contractions throughout. Look at the motto of *The New York*

Times: "All the news that's fit to print." Some people say, "Newspapers. So what?" Well, in my experience, most newspaper editors try very hard to use a correct yet readable style. They're often a good source for usage. But, also, most other writing you enjoy—like books you pay money for—uses plain English, complete with contractions.

One agency I worked with, however, just couldn't bring itself to use contractions. We finally got to plain English, but we had to take the long way around.

Here's what happened: When people who weren't used to writing plain English tried writing without contractions, their writing reverted to typical legalese. They stopped talking on paper. So we had them start over, writing their *drafts* with contractions. The writing improved.

Then, after writing with contractions, the writers simply *un*contracted later (with help from computers). The result was plain English. But, I confess: the tone was rather stiff.

Tip

Try a contraction in the next thing you write. The first time, you may feel uncomfortable. But go ahead. You'll soon feel free, as though a burden has fallen from your shoulders as you begin to write.

What about the rules we learned in school?

At this point, you may be wondering if we should pay attention to anything we learned in school. That depends on the school, because many are terrific. And, of course, we need to follow certain rules or else communication will become hopelessly erratic.

There are three categories of rules to consider:

- rules we all agree with
- rules few people agree with
- rules amateurs follow and professionals don't

Let's look more closely at each of these.

Rules we all agree with

Some rules just aren't controversial. For example, we all know to start sentences with capital letters and end them with periods or other terminal marks of punctuation. We also want subjects to agree with verbs and pronouns to agree with the nouns they replace. There aren't really a lot of these rules that cause us a problem. For the most part, people in business know them and follow them.

Rules few people agree with

There's another category of rules "experts" on language try to foist on us. Jim Quinn, author of *American Tongue and Cheek,* calls these "experts" pop grammarians—people who seem to have a stone tablet from God filled with "The Commandments" on usage.

One of those pop grammarians, according to Quinn, is Edwin Newman, author of *Strictly Speaking.* In *Strictly Speaking,* Newman is appalled by the construction *convince to* (as in "The Soviet Union evidently is not able to *convince* Cairo *to* accept a rapid cease-fire.").

In all my teaching and consulting, I've never found another soul who agrees with Newman on that issue. Yet he calls it "one of the worst things" *The New York Times* does.

Don't worry about the pop grammarians. They're talking—and mainly arguing—only with each other. Virtually all linguists, the real experts on language, disagree with the pop grammarians.

Rules amateurs follow and professionals don't

Professionals *are* professionals because readers pay for what they write. (How much would you pay for the stuff in your in-box?)

Professionals follow the standard rules (such as beginning sentences with capital letters); they ignore almost all of the rules by the pop grammarians; and they ignore a few rules they learned in school.

What are the rules from school the professionals have learned to ignore? John Trimble, in his classic book *Writing with Style: Conversations on the Art of Writing*, lists "The Seven Nevers":

The Seven Nevers [from decades past]

1. Never begin a sentence with *and* or *but.*

2. Never use contractions.

3. Never refer to the reader as *you.*

4. Never use the first person pronoun *I.*

5. Never end a sentence with a preposition.

6. Never split an infinitive.

7. Never write a paragraph containing only a single sentence.

Trimble then says he's going to argue against all of them, "earnestly hoping that I may free you of their hold forever."

I agree. The Seven Nevers would be good rules only with a key revision. You guessed it—strike out the word *never:*

1. ~~Never~~ begin a sentence with *and* or *but.*

2. ~~Never~~ use contractions.

3. ~~Never~~ refer to the reader as *you.*

4. ~~Never~~ use the first person pronoun *I.*

5. ~~Never~~ end a sentence with a preposition.

6. ~~Never~~ split an infinitive.

7. ~~Never~~ write a paragraph containing only a single sentence.

That's what almost all professionals have learned to do. Again, just look at professional writing, and you'll see you've been reading spoken English—plain English—complete with split infinitives, one-sentence paragraphs, and sentences ending with prepositions. Just the way we talk.

And check your grammar handbook. You may be surprised to find that almost all handbooks agree with Trimble—and discourage those old-fashioned and destructive "Seven Nevers."

So remember the most important lesson on style: write the way you talk! It's much easier—on your reader and on you.

You'll learn more about style in these chapters:

- Chapter 6, "Passive voice"

- Chapter 7, "Abstractness"

- Chapter 8, "Punctuation"

For now, though, let's turn to the second major part of plain English writing: organization.

CHAPTER 3

Organization: getting to the point

Bottom line

Make your main point easy to find.

My key advice on organization is simple: start with your main point. Tell your readers, right at the start:

- what you want them to do ("I recommend you buy a color printer")

- what your conclusion is ("Wages will increase next year"), or

- whatever your main purpose is for your document

Now, the main point doesn't have to be the first sentence (though it can be much of the time). I'm just saying that the main point should be up front—*before* your reasons instead of after.

Why do you want the main point first?

What happens if you're reading something ten pages long and the main point is *not* up front? I think most of us get confused and frustrated, so we skip to the end and hunt for it. Once we find it, we can usually start over and understand the document much better. With the context of the bottom line, the details up front start to make more sense to us.

So why do writers often put the main point at the end? Here are some common reasons I've heard:

- to make readers read the entire document
- to build the case so readers will more likely accept the main point
- to reenact how the writer learned something
- to delay bad news

Those reasons all sound good, don't they? The problem is, as I've already noted, most readers simply don't put up with that order. We'll stop reading, skip to the end, get the bottom line, and then (if the writer's lucky), start in again at the top.

Even bad news should normally come early. You don't necessarily make it the first sentence: "You're fired." But that kind of news shouldn't follow a page and a half of the company's financial situation, either, should it?

Also, with bad news, tone becomes extremely important. You probably want to say something with a less rude tone than: "You're fired."

There are a number of ways to deliver the same message with a polite tone, and that message needs to be earlier rather than later.

First example: the auditors have come!

Suppose you've just had outside auditors look over your financial records. They've spent three months with access to all your files and all your people. Today they hand you their report. Do you want to plow through all their facts—

everything they examined—to find that your company looks great? Or that one of your division managers has been cheating? Wouldn't you rather have the conclusion up front?

For instance, consider these two good starts for audit reports (each with the bottom line up front):

> After three months of examining your records for the past year, we have found no major discrepancies.
>
> *or*
>
> After three months of examining your records for the past year, we have found the following:
>
> • Your marketing division is systematically hiding its losses each month—totaling $300,000 for the past 6 months alone.
>
> • The division manager and her assistant appear to be the only people involved.
>
> • There were no other major discrepancies.

Notice that starting with the main point doesn't mean saying only what you're going to cover: "This report tells you the results of the audit we've been conducting for the past three months." No, starting with the main point means telling what you found. Starting with only the topic simply isn't enough—just as a table of contents usually isn't enough to serve as the summary of a book.

Second example: the letter in the in-box

Don't you wonder, with every piece of paper in your in-box, "Does this ask me to *do* anything?" And don't you wish the writer would start with that—and then tell you why? Even with short memos and letters, most of us appreciate getting the main point early. For example, what if you're having a busy day as personnel director for your company, and this comes in from an employment agency:

> Dear Max:
>
> On December 15, I received a phone call from Mr. Jason Brown from Michigan, who was your director of sailing in the Saginaw school. Mr. Brown, who recently had a fine interview with us, has requested I contact you. He requests a letter of verification of employment, including confirmation of his job title and the duties he performed while in your school. According to Mr. Brown, he needs this to apply for a similar position in the Caribbean.
>
> I would appreciate your help in this matter.
>
> Sincerely,

What's the key sentence buried in that letter? It's the one asking for the verification of employment. You can find it without experiencing major frustration, but wouldn't you have preferred the request first—like this:

> Dear Max:
>
> Would you verify the employment of Mr. Jason Brown?
>
> Mr. Brown was your director of sailing in the Saginaw school [then give the rest of the details]. . . .
>
> Sincerely,

Better, isn't it?

Tip

For the next memo or letter you write, ask yourself, "Am I asking my reader to do anything?" If you are, try starting with that request—and put it in the form of a question (as in the example you just read).

Third example: where's that color printer???

At the beginning of the chapter, I mentioned that one reason writers put the main point last is to reenact how they learned something. In fact, I think that's probably the most common reason of all. Writers simply use the same order on paper in which events actually occurred.

Suppose, for example, you've been spending the last few days ordering a new printer for your office. Your boss says to you, "How about sending me a memo and letting me know where things stand." You might be tempted to organize your memo by chronology—the way things happened:

> On July 7, you asked me to order a color printer for our office. On that same day, I contacted Cameron Melton (our computer expert) and began coordinating our request with him. Cameron told me that we have the funds and that the kind of printer we want is on the authorized list. Therefore, Cameron gave us permission to make the buy.
>
> On July 9, I called the printer company and found out the exact price ($3,799). Later that day, I contacted Laura in purchasing. Together, Laura and I filled out the request for the printer.
>
> On July 11, Mackenzie okayed the order and sent it to the printer company.
>
> On July 14, I confirmed that the printer company received our order. The salesperson I spoke with said we will have the printer by 9:30 a.m. tomorrow.

Takes forever to get to the bottom line, doesn't it? You can see, though, that the writer simply followed the chronology of what happened, tracking the purchase step by step for the boss.

Writers are often tempted by chronological order. But what does the boss really want to know? Certainly not a blow-by-blow account of the process. Remember, the request was this: "Let me know where things stand." Keeping that in mind, let's try a different start:

> We'll be getting our color printer by 9:30 a.m. tomorrow. It will cost $3,799.
>
> Approval was simple: Cameron Melton (our computer expert) authorized it quickly. Laura (in purchasing) was very helpful preparing the order. Jason okayed the order and sent it out without incident.

Notice that the second memo gets right to the point: the printer is coming tomorrow. Notice also that the memo is much shorter. That often happens. When you begin with your main point, you're much less likely to put in anything irrelevant. In fact, you might not even need the second paragraph.

✢   ✢   ✢

So starting with the main point helps keep your reader on track—and *you* (the writer), too.

You'll learn more about organization in these chapters:

- Chapter 9, "Blueprint"
- Chapter 10, "Executive summary"

Now let's look at the last of the three parts of plain English writing: layout.

CHAPTER 4

Layout: adding visual impact

Bottom line

<u>Show</u> *your reader the underlying structure of your writing by using headings, lists, and other good techniques of white space.*

When I give presentations on writing, my audiences usually consider layout to be the most important topic I cover.

What is layout, anyway? On its simplest level, it is whatever goes into the "look" of the page: something that appears open and inviting probably has good layout; something that appears cluttered and *un*inviting probably has bad layout.

The look of a page is important, but we'll see that good layout has two other terrific advantages:

- Good layout shows the reader—visually—your organization.

- It also helps you—the writer—be organized in the first place.

Layout is much more than packaging a document: it is the driving force behind organization. People who are aware of the techniques of good layout almost always write with good organization.

In this chapter, I'll suggest three layout techniques:

- Use short paragraphs.

- Use headings.

- Use bullets and other lists.

These techniques are important at all times and *absolutely crucial* when the content of your writing is complex—as business writing often is.

Let's look at each of these techniques in more detail.

Use short paragraphs

Too often, the standard layout for business writing is wall-to-wall words. You've no doubt seen such pages. They look something like this (the gray part represents text):

One big paragraph—not very appealing, is it?

Now let's make the layout a *little* better by simply changing the shape of the words—arranging them into more paragraphs:

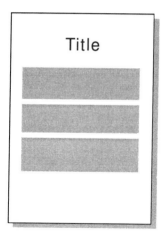

Looks better, doesn't it? And, of course, the paragraphs can be even shorter than these.

A question often comes up about this time: "But isn't a paragraph a paragraph? Can we start paragraphs just anywhere?"

We can't start paragraphs anywhere, but there are many options. The old (un)truism is this: "Each paragraph should represent a separate thought. Some thoughts take longer than others; therefore, some paragraphs may be very long."

To some extent, paragraphs do represent separate thoughts, but what is a "thought," anyway? Every sentence contains at least one thought and probably several. True, a new paragraph can signal the next major thought, but business writing has a better technique: headings.

If you use headings—and I highly recommend them—you can paragraph almost visually beneath them. The headings show the boundaries of the major "thoughts."

Also, think about newspapers—just how long are their paragraphs? Their paragraphs are short—because long paragraphs would be quite forbidding in narrow newspaper columns.

In fact, if you give the same text to a newspaper editor and to a textbook editor to divide into paragraphs, you'd get different results: the newspaper editor would give you many short paragraphs; the textbook editor would give you longer ones (because textbook columns are much wider). In other words, both editors would paragraph—to some extent—visually. And that's what I recommend you do, too. Now let's look at a related topic.

Use headings

Just using short paragraphs isn't good enough. You also need to *show* your organization—visually—to your readers. A good way to do that is with headings. Think of headings as "labels" for the parts of your document.

For example, the memo we just worked with has short paragraphs, but it doesn't have labels for the various parts. Let's improve it one more step by adding those "labels":

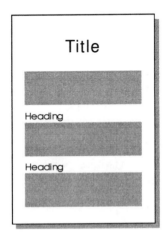

Tip _____

> *Make your headings actually communicate with your reader (such as "When will the new computers arrive?" instead of "computers"). And feel free to have more than one paragraph below a heading.*

As you can see, headings are an important key to good business writing. They can also help you as a supervisor of writers. Suppose, for example, you're managing a large writing project. If you ask your people to use headings when they write, you know what you'll get? Not just headings, but organization, too. It's hard for people to use headings without being organized.

Headings are the "little thing that does the big thing": a technique of layout that forces good organization. At the very least, headings require people to arrange their document into blocks of information instead of scattering ideas throughout. Headings also often keep people from using a chronological organization, which, because it often buries the main point, usually isn't appropriate.

Use bullets and other indented lists

Headings are terrific—and so are indented lists. As you can tell, I seldom write more than a page or so without using them somewhere. Just as headings show organization for the blocks of information in a document, lists often show organization within paragraphs.

A quick example: the value of lists

Business writing often has lists in it somewhere, and organized writers use lists particularly often. A list is all right as part of the text of a paragraph, but it's usually more effective if it's indented.

For example, read this sentence:

> Three satellites are in geosynchronous orbit at 23,000 miles over the equator: Satellite I is at 55 degrees west longitude, Satellite II is at 70 degrees west longitude, and Satellite III is at 140 degrees west longitude.

Next, see how much better the layout is when we indent the list:

> Three satellites are in geosynchronous orbit at 23,000 miles over the equator:
>
> - Satellite I is at 55 degrees west longitude.
> - Satellite II is at 70 degrees west longitude.
> - Satellite III is at 140 degrees west longitude.

Indenting with bullets helps untangle that technical information.

A second example: bullets or numbers?

Here's another example—a set of instructions—that could benefit from indented lists:

> To set up this laptop computer, you must take the following steps. Push the dual latches mounted on top of the computer outward to release the top/monitor assembly. Move the top/monitor assembly to an oblique angle with the unit's base. Push the release switch on Disk Drive A away from you to release the drive.

This paragraph is well organized, but it doesn't look it. The problem is ineffective layout. So let's take a first step to improve the layout by using bullets—notice the difference already:

To set up this laptop computer, you must take the following steps:

- Push the dual latches mounted on top of the computer outward to release the top/monitor assembly.

- Move the top/monitor assembly to an oblique angle with the unit's base.

- Push the release switch on Disk Drive A away from you to release the drive.

The paragraph now isolates each step visually. Notice that all bulleted items begin the same way grammatically (in this case, with verbs). That's good. The grammatical term for that is "parallelism."

Even though the layout is much better for that paragraph (visually revealing the good organization that was already there), there's still a better way: a numbered list.

I suggest numbered lists when you're giving steps; otherwise, use bulleted lists (to give a unified look to the pages of your document). So my final solution would be a numbered list, like this:

To set up this laptop computer, you must take the following steps:

1. Push the dual latches mounted on top of the computer outward to release the top/monitor assembly.

2. Move the top/monitor assembly to an oblique angle with the unit's base.

3. Push the release switch on Disk Drive A away from you to release the drive.

Do you see the advantage of good layout? It helps readers see a document's organization: the headings label the blocks of information; the indented lists isolate the facts, steps, arguments.

Even more important, good layout helps *produce* good organization. Writers who are aware of the techniques of good layout think about it *as* they write, not afterward. And as they write, they naturally form their ideas into blocks of information, and they isolate many of their facts, steps, and arguments into lists.

You'll learn more about layout in these chapters:

- Chapter 11, "Typefaces"
- Chapter 12, "Headings"
- Chapter 13, "Bullets"
- Chapter 14, "Graphics"

Now let's turn to the final chapter in this section. It puts everything together in a model.

CHAPTER 5

A model for writing

Bottom line

There's a simple model that can help you get started with a lot of your business writing.

This chapter presents a model you can use for much of your business writing—a "template" that will hold the ideas in many documents. These documents can be short (like memos) or long (like reports or even books).

If this sounds too good to be true, it isn't. I've used this model—or variations—many times, including for some of the most challenging and complex writing in government and business, writing involving complicated documents by auditors, lawyers, and accountants.

Basically, the model says to:

- start with your main point

- organize your writing into blocks of information

- label those blocks with headings so your readers can see where blocks start and end

The model is simple. And it seems obvious. But how often do you see writing that actually follows it? Once you try it, you'll see how often you can use it.

It's simple and effective!

A model for writing

First, let's look at an illustration of what the model *isn't:*

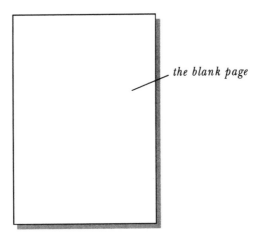

the blank page

The blank page! Now let's look at the model:

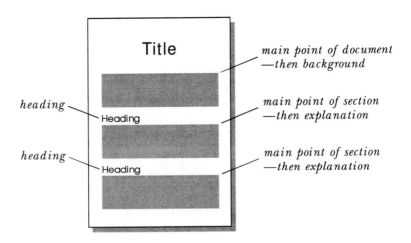

*main point of document
—then background*

*main point of section
—then explanation*

*main point of section
—then explanation*

And here's an explanation of the model:

1. Begin with your main point: whatever you want your reader to do or understand.

2. Organize your content into sections—or blocks—of related information. Those blocks don't have to be single paragraphs—they could be pages long (broken into short paragraphs, of course).

3. Label each of those blocks with a heading. Use subheadings, too, if the blocks are long.

4. Try to start each block by stating its main point. For example, if your heading is a question, begin the block by answering that question.

5. And use details—sometimes in bulleted lists—to support that main point.

Simple, isn't it?

The model in action

Let's apply the model. Here, as an example, is the beginning of a memo:

> This memo asks for your authorization to rent three computers for $900 total cost.
>
> We've ordered three personal computers to work on the Laredo project, but the supplier can't get them to us until June 1. Because we must start the project sooner, we need to rent other computers in the meantime. This memo gives you the details.
>
> **Why are our new computers late?**
> The manufacturer had trouble with defective computer chips. As a result. . . . [The memo then continues with

more explanation in this paragraph and more sections with headings.]

Notice that:

- The first paragraph is the main point of the document: I want you to pay $900 to rent computers.

- There are headings to label the blocks of information in the body of the document. This example, which shows only the beginning of the memo, has the heading, "Why are our new computers late?"

- The first sentence after the heading is the main point of the section: the manufacturer had trouble with computer chips.

You can see this model can help untangle complex information for the reader—and for the writer. If you aim for this model when you begin writing, starting will be easier, and you'll be more organized.

Does this model seem mechanical? Yes, it is. Too mechanical? I doubt it. The content of business writing can become extraordinarily complex; at the same time, readers are often busy. A mechanical organization is a blessing for a busy reader (for busy writers, too).

Think about yourself around April 15 each year. What kind of organization do you want for the instructions on filling out your income tax forms? If you're like me, you want the organization to be *absolutely clear*—with no ambiguity whatsoever.

Does the model work all the time?

No—not all the time.

It works especially well for busy readers who want to get information as quickly as possible and then move on to something else. It works for people who *have* to read whatever you're writing and want the writing to be as painless as possible.

It doesn't work as well when you need to engage readers creatively and hold their attention with an entertaining style or innovative organization. Frankly, most people enjoy that kind of writing off the job but don't enjoy it on the job. They see the creative part as a waste of time (I don't, but I've found I'm in the minority).

Again, think of yourself as a reader: how much of the writing you read could benefit by following this model?

Does the model work for technical writing?

Yes, the model works *especially* well for technical, complex writing. In fact, the more complex the writing is, the more important this model is for the reader. But just because the model works for complex writing doesn't mean it isn't suited for simple explanations and recommendations, too. The example in this chapter—about renting a computer— is relatively simple, and the model serves it well.

Do you need to follow all parts of the model?

No, you don't need to follow all parts of the model all the time. For example, sometimes you might want to give the reader a little background before you can make your main point—either for the entire document or part of it.

You must still be careful, though, to keep the background to a minimum before you get to the point. Remember: readers know how to skip ahead.

When I have a lot of background to cover, I try to give the minimum up front, then state the main point, then add background if necessary. But a funny thing happens when I get the main point up front: I find I need much less background than I thought.

So keep the model in mind *before* and *as* you write. It's simple and effective.

✣   ✣   ✣

You've now read about each of the key parts of writing in plain English:

- style: writing the way you talk
- organization: getting to the point
- layout: adding visual impact

The next three sections tell you more about each of those parts.

MORE ABOUT
STYLE

CHAPTER 6

Passive voice

Bottom line

Use active voice—unless you have a <u>strong</u> reason to use passive.

This chapter attacks the most important villain of readability in business and technical writing: passive voice.

If you've heard one outcry against bad business and government writing, it's "Too much passive voice!" That's a good outcry, because bureaucratic writers significantly overuse it. Passive voice isn't always bad, but lots of it absolutely kills readability.

What is passive voice?

Identifying passive voice is simple. Just go through these two steps:

1. Look for a form of the verb *to be*. Here's the complete list: *am, are, is, was, were, be, been, being.*

2. Now look for a past participle. These are easy to identify: they normally end in *-ed* or *-en*. Examples: *carri<u>ed</u>, tak<u>en</u>.* Note: There are a few irregular verbs that have past participles that don't end in *-ed* or *-en*: *held, made, kept,* etc. You'll soon get the hang of identifying them.

If both parts are present, you have passive voice. Here's an example:

$$\text{The box } \underbrace{\text{was}}_{\text{form of the verb } \underline{to\ be}} \text{lifted by the worker.}$$

form of the verb to be

The box was lifted by the worker.

AND a past participle

Here are some other examples of verbs in the passive voice:

has *been* fitt*ed*

could have *been* tak*en*

were writt*en*

is done (irregular verb)

are kept (irregular verb)

Notice that you can always add a prepositional phrase beginning with *by* to passive sentences:

The suit has been fitted *by the tailor*.

The report is kept *by the analysts*.

Easy enough, isn't it? So just look for:

- a form of the verb *to be*
- *and* a past participle

If you have both, you have a verb that's passive. And because you have a passive verb, there will always be a slot for a prepositional phrase beginning with *by*.

So where does the name "passive" come from?

Sentences with passive voice have a subject that's "passive." That is, the subject isn't doing whatever the verb says. It's not the actor; instead, it's acted upon.

In this sentence, for example, the subject ("the ball") is passive. It's acted upon:

	subject
Passive voice:	The ball was tossed by Elizabeth.
	acted upon **ACTOR**

Now let's turn things around and make the sentence active:

	subject
Active voice:	Elizabeth tossed the ball.
	ACTOR *acted upon*

The subject ("Elizabeth") is now active. It's doing what the verb says: tossing.

What's the difference: voice and tense?

Some people confuse passive voice and past tense. They think they have to use passive voice because something happened in the past. No. *Passive* voice and *past* tense may sound alike, but they're completely different.

Here's a verb with passive voice and past tense:

The file cabinet was moved.

And here's proof we don't need to use passive voice for something that happened in the past:

The contractor moved the file cabinet.

That sentence is still past tense but now in active voice.

Voice, as we've seen, refers to whether or not the subject is the actor in the sentence. *Tense*, on the other hand, simply refers to the time an action takes place (past, present, future). So you can have any combination of voice and tense.

What's the matter with passive voice?

Passive voice isn't wrong, but it often causes problems. That's because it often leaves out information that the reader needs. Let me explain how that happens—usually unconsciously by the writer. Remember I said that passive sentences always have a slot for a prepositional phrase beginning with *by*?

> The policy has been approved by the CEO.

> or

> The policy has been approved.

In the first sentence, the words in the *by* phrase (showing the actor) are actually there; in the second, they aren't there, but there's a place—a slot—for them. Both sentences, of course, are passive.

Too often, passive sentences in business writing are like the second sentence: they leave out the *by* phrase (and, consequently, the actor). Sometimes you, the reader, can guess who the actor is; sometimes you can't. For example, look at this sentence:

> When a computer file has *been created*, it must *be moved* to the remote node.

Sounds simple, even though it's passive, doesn't it? But what does it mean? Notice that it has left out both *by* phases (and both actors):

> When a computer file has been created [by ???], it must be moved [by ???] to the remote node.

So we have to guess who—or what—the actors are: Is the *user* creating the computer file? Probably—but we're guessing. And who is moving the computer file? The user? The system administrator? The system itself? Unless we already know what this writer is talking about, we must guess.

Well, this sentence came from a writer I was working with. Here's what he wrote when I asked him to put the sentence into active voice:

> When a *user* creates a computer file, the *system* must move it to the remote node.

Just check your in-box. Find a piece of writing that's hard to read. And then notice how many passives leave out the *by* phrase—and leave you guessing who is doing the action.

Why do people write passive voice?

One reason people write passive voice is to *intentionally* leave out the actor. For example, timid bosses wouldn't want to write this sentence:

> I have decided everybody must work this weekend.

The actor is *I*—who may seem pretty exposed to gripes and other criticism from the people who can't go sailing or skiing during the weekend. So some bureaucrats, to avoid responsibility, tend to put such a sentence in passive voice and then eliminate the *by* prepositional phrase:

> It has been determined ~~by me~~ that you must work this weekend.

Now, through the magic of passive voice, the boss is in the clear. After all, who can find the subject of that sentence—"It"—to gripe to?

But this reason—avoiding responsibility—actually accounts for only a small percentage of the sentences in passive voice. After all, only a few key sentences in any document are ones in which people must accept or avoid responsibility.

A second reason people write passively is that they try to avoid using personal pronouns like *we* and *you*. However, unless they use personal pronouns, passive voice is the natural result.

So pronouns are the key. In fact, bosses who say, "Write in plain English, but don't use any personal pronouns," are like home builders who say, "Build me a nice house, but—hey—I don't like hammers, so don't use them." Hard to build a house without hammers, and hard to write plain English without pronouns.

And a third reason people write passively? They just do. They start in passive voice and then just stay in passive voice. Without much effort at all, they could easily have written the same ideas actively.

Is passive voice ever all right?

Of course. At least three times:

- when you don't know the actor ("John was murdered.")

- when the actor is unimportant to the point you're making ("The senator was reelected.")

- when the emphasis is clearly not on the actor but on the acted upon ("What happened to the little girl? *The little girl* was rescued.")

So don't think of passive voice as always bad. Think of it as putting unnecessary strain on the reader. Use passive when you need to—but be careful of overusing it. Seldom have readers suffered because writers overused *active* voice.

Tip

Work hard to use active voice. Try to use passive only as a relatively uncommon exception.

❖   ❖   ❖

Is writing active voice worth the effort? Absolutely! It can make a dramatic impact on the readability of your writing. In fact, if you habitually write passive voice, I can almost guarantee that your readers have been skimming in frustration and confusion.

Do you want to find out if you're writing passive voice? Take some of your recent business writing and circle all the passives on one full page. If you find only two or three, you're doing fine. If, on the other hand, you find many more . . .

Some of today's grammar checkers can tell you what percentage of your verbs are in passive voice. I average under 3% in this book. You should definitely be under 10% for most of your writing.

Now let's turn to another serious problem of business writing: abstractness. It's almost as serious a problem as passive voice.

CHAPTER 7

Abstractness

Bottom line

Keep your reader from guessing what you mean—by using examples, brief stories, and comparisons.

This chapter helps you conquer another villain of readability: abstractness. Let's begin by defining it.

What is abstract writing?

Abstract writing is so general that readers constantly have to guess what it means. If I stopped there, that sentence would be abstract—you'd have to guess what *I* mean. So let's consider an example. Here's an abstract sentence:

> As a property manager, I sometimes find strange things.

It's hard to picture exactly what the writer means. Things can be "strange" in different ways. We're left, to some extent, to guess exactly what the writer means by that word.

As a result, the sentence isn't memorable. By memorable, I don't mean deathless prose such as "Give me liberty or give me death!" I simply mean something we can remember by the time we finish the page. Abstract sentences don't pass the "memorable" test.

So abstract writing is writing that is ambiguous and hard for us to picture.

The opposite of "abstract" is "concrete." So let's move beyond the abstract sentence I just showed you by adding a concrete illustration:

> As a property manager, I sometimes find strange things. At one property, I found two people living in an electrical room (the room housing electrical meters). They worked at the property and lived in the closet . . . mostly trying to avoid a long commute.

The illustration helps us visualize what the writer means by "strange." As a result, the passage has moved from abstract to concrete. It isn't deathless prose, but we'll probably remember it well after we turn the page. The concreteness helps it become more memorable.

Abstract writing, then, is so vague that it asks us to stop reading and guess what it means. Normally we don't do that. Instead, we just keep reading, hoping for something better in the next sentence or the next paragraph. If there isn't anything better, we might just go to lunch.

Even if we make educated guesses to figure out the abstract writing, we can't be sure we've gotten the author's intended meaning. That's why professional writers take the guesswork out by supplying the missing information.

How can you be more concrete?

Concreteness is crucial to good writing. The rest of the chapter looks at these three ways to be more concrete:

- Use quick examples.
- Tell brief stories.
- Make comparisons.

Use quick examples

A quick example is normally fairly short—from a word to a couple of sentences. Here are three:

> As a loan officer, I will not hesitate to hold up an application of a member whose salary I question. *For example, I would be suspicious of someone who is eighteen and makes $50,000.*

•   •   •

> I am responsible for making sure the computer system is running smoothly every day. If there are any problems—*such as a database running out of space*—I am called to fix it.

•   •   •

> We answer over 100 questions a day from federal employees about our program to offer them incentives to resign. *For example, employees often call to find out if they are eligible. We received one call from a wife whose husband had taken the buyout. She had put up with him at home for a week and had had enough. She wanted his agency to take him back!*

Lists are another good place for quick examples. For instance, auditors try to find out whether things are going well within an organization. If they find something wrong, that something is a "finding." This list tells auditors what a report of a finding should cover:

> These are the five elements of a finding you must cover in your report:
>
> 1. condition
>
> 2. cause
>
> 3. criteria
>
> 4. effect
>
> 5. recommendation

Abstract. Now for the concrete. Let's put in some quick examples:

> These are the five elements of a finding you must cover in your report:
>
>   1. *Condition.* Example: The nurses don't record the medicine they give their patients.
>
>   2. *Cause.* Example: The nursing staff is 42% short of people, leaving little time for nurses to both give the medicine and record that they've given it.
>
>   3. *Criteria.* Example: Hospital Regulation 213.4 says that whoever gives medicine must record that fact.
>
>   4. *Effect.* Example: Patients could die or have worsened conditions if they receive too much or too little medicine.
>
>   5. *Recommendation.* Example: Counsel all nurses and require supervisors to monitor the records.

You certainly noticed that the concrete version is longer. That's true. But longer is not necessarily worse. The real issue is, "Which version communicates more efficiently to the reader?" Sometimes more writing is better than less.

You may wonder when you should use quick examples. The answer: whenever your reader won't understand the abstract version alone. Professional writers use them frequently.

Tip

A good suggestion for supervisors is to tell your people to use lots of these two transitions (or words like them): for instance and for example. The result will almost always be more concreteness. And concreteness translates to information that readers remember.

Tell brief stories

We all love stories. What's our reaction when a speaker says, "Let me tell you what happened last Saturday evening"? Our ears perk up, and we suddenly pay attention.

The same thing happens to readers—a story perks them up. Consider this one:

> Part of my job is to help low-income families. For example, a family of three (soon to be four) moved from a homeless shelter to an apartment. The only things they brought with them were the clothes on their backs.
>
> The manager of the property asked me to help this family with utilities, clothing, furniture, and food. So I called the electric and phone companies to give them information about the family.
>
> Once the companies processed the information, the electricity and phone began to work. The next thing was to find clothes and furniture. The family and I went to the Salvation Army. We found some good quality clothes and good pieces of furniture to take back to their apartment.
>
> Finally, I showed them where the nearest grocery store was and how to use food stamps.

See how the story helps make something abstract—helping others—more memorable? Sometimes, for an important point, the extra words a story requires are well worth the reader's time.

Make comparisons

If there's one technique of concreteness that separates amateurs from professionals, it's that professionals tend to use many comparisons.

However, comparisons have a plus and a minus:

- *The plus.* A good comparison will probably be the most memorable part of a piece of writing.

- *The minus.* A good comparison is hard to think of.

Nevertheless, many people have thought of excellent ones. John D. MacDonald, a famous novelist, used comparisons often in his writing. Here's one from *The Dreadful Lemon Sky* telling us about news stories:

> But a news story is a fragile thing. *It is like a hot air balloon. It needs a constant additive of more hot air in the form of new revelations, new actions, new suspicions. Without this the air cools, the big bag wrinkles, sighs, settles to the ground, and disappears.*

We know that comparisons appear in novels, but do they appear in business writing? Yes. Here's a good one about "client-serving computing":

> A common use for client-serving computing is for processing large amounts of data. For example, if you need to produce a huge personnel report, you can have a powerful computer come up with the data for the report (doing the number crunching and sorting), and you can put the data on a less powerful computer to format the report. *In this case, it's like digging a ditch with a backhoe to dig up the heavy dirt and then using shovels to even out the edges of the hole.*

So check your writing for abstractness. Are there places you could add quick examples? Brief stories? Comparisons? Your writing may grow a bit longer, but it will probably communicate much better.

Now let's look at the final chapter on style: punctuation. It can make a big difference in your writing.

CHAPTER 8

Punctuation

Bottom line

Use colons, dashes, semicolons, question marks, and other punctuation to replace the voice inflection and hand gestures we use when we talk.

Punctuation has intimidated brave men and women for years. Yet it's not that hard—really. This chapter simplifies some rules and makes them easier to learn.

How often is punctuation important when you write? The answer: every time. So take a few minutes now to expand your arsenal. There's no need to spend the rest of your life restricted to only the period, the comma, and the colon introducing a list.

This chapter gives a few new ways to look at colons, dashes, and semicolons.

Why is punctuation important?

Imagine, if you will, a string of words with no punctuation whatsoever:

    XX XXXX XXX XXXXX XX X XXXXXXXXX XXXX XX X XXXXXXX XXXX
    XX X XXXX XXXXXX XXX XXXXXX XX XXXXXXXXXX XXX XXXX
    XXXXXX XXX XXXX XXXX XX XXXXXXXXXXX

There's a misconception that someone who is good at punctuation simply knows what punctuation mark should go where: a comma here, a semicolon there, a period at the end.

However, for someone who is good at punctuation, the words come out differently than for someone who is not. People who understand commas, semicolons, periods—and especially colons, dashes, and question marks—produce entirely different sentence structures from people who are not good at punctuation.

The result? Better sentences that have the emphasis—and ideas—in just the right places.

So don't think of punctuation as a way to go *wrong* (as a way to make mistakes). Instead, think of punctuation as a way to go *right*—as a way to say just what you mean in the best way possible.

Please note: This chapter gives you only a few of the most common and useful rules for colons, dashes, and semicolons. If you follow these rules, you will produce correct punctuation. But don't "correct" other people's writing just because they don't follow the rules here. There are other correct ways I don't include. (For a more complete look at punctuation, see any of the various handbooks on writing.)

The colon

General definition of the colon

The colon is an extremely useful mark of punctuation. Think of it as an "arrow" that comes at the end of a complete sentence, pointing to some more useful information about what you just said. The colon can "point" to a word, to a list, to a sentence, even to a series of sentences or paragraphs.

Rules for the colon

1. Use a colon (after a complete sentence) to point to a single word:

   • He started the business for one reason: money.

2. Use a colon (after a complete sentence) to point to a list:

   • He started the business for three reasons: adventure, fame, and money.

3. Use a colon (after a complete sentence) to point to another complete sentence:

   • He had always been a thrill-seeker: he once climbed the northwest face of Half Dome.

4. Use a colon (after a complete sentence) to point to a series of sentences or paragraphs:

   • He started the business for three reasons: He wanted adventure. He wanted fame. He wanted money.

Notice in each of these cases that the part after the colon receives emphasis. For instance, what's the difference between these two sentences?

   • He started the business because he wanted money.

   • He started the business for one reason: money.

Emphasis! The word *money* in the second sentence seems to have a spotlight on it.

Now—which is the better sentence? We can't say, can we? It depends on context and how much emphasis we want to give to *money*.

But who is the better writer: the one who can write both kinds of sentences or the one who can write only the one without the colon? Probably the one who writes both kinds is better because that person has more tools to control emphasis.

Now let's look at another important mark for plain English—the dash.

The dash

General definition of the dash

Like the colon, the dash is an extremely useful mark of punctuation. It tells the reader that you are saying "something more" about what you just said—an example, an elaboration, a contradiction, whatever.

Handbooks once discouraged the dash as too informal for business writing; today we see the old books as too formal for plain English. Now the dash is a fully accredited mark of punctuation.

Tip

> *Use a dash in the next thing you write. If you haven't been using a dash in your business writing before, you'll find it to be remarkably handy for emphasizing your important ideas.*

Rules for the dash

1. Use a dash as you would a colon: as an "arrow" that comes at the end of a complete sentence, pointing to some more useful information about what you just said. Notice that the dash gives a slightly more informal feel to the sentence than a colon does:

   • He started the business for one reason—money.

   • He started the business for three reasons—adventure, fame, and money.

- He had always been a thrill-seeker—he once climbed the northwest face of Half Dome.

Normally you shouldn't use the dash to point to a series of sentences or paragraphs.

2. Use a pair of dashes (one on each side) to set off useful information in the middle of a sentence:

- He robbed the bank—the one just around the corner—for the sheer adventure.

The sentence is, "He robbed the bank for the sheer adventure." The phrase "the one just around the corner" is in the middle of the sentence.

Question: What three marks could you put around that phrase?

Answer: a set of commas, a set of dashes, or a set of parentheses.

The difference? Dashes add emphasis to the phrase, commas give standard emphasis, and parentheses treat it like a whispered aside.

3. Use a dash (even where you might have no other punctuation) to emphasize the last idea in a sentence:

- He robbed the bank—for adventure, notoriety, and greed.
- He robbed the bank for adventure, notoriety—and greed.

Again, you can see the effect the dash has on emphasis.

The semicolon

General definition of the semicolon

The semicolon is more formal than the colon and the dash. Professional writers today tend to use it much less than writers of several decades ago did.

Some people think of the semicolon as a "strong comma"—something between a comma and a period. That's true, but it's not the whole story.

The semicolon also has to separate equal grammatical units—an independent clause from another independent clause, or a dependent clause from another dependent clause, or a phrase from a phrase. The semicolon does not separate unequal units—like an *in*dependent clause from a *de*pendent clause.

In other words, think of the semicolon as a kind of "pivot": one idea is on this side of the semicolon; another idea is on that side of it. And on each side of the pivot point is a similar grammatical unit.

Rules for the semicolon

1. Use a semicolon to join two (or more) complete sentences to show that those sentences are closely related.

   • In spring, the blossoms are beautiful on the apple trees; in autumn, the apples are a nuisance on the lawn.

   You may wonder how the semicolon is different from a colon or dash, which can also separate two sentences. The difference has to do with the second sentence, the one after the colon, dash, or semicolon. For the colon and dash, the second sentence is usually an example or elaboration; for the semicolon, the second sentence is usually a similar or opposite idea (as in this sentence). If this seems a bit fuzzy, you're right: there aren't clear rights and wrongs.

   Now here's another example of a semicolon separating two sentences:

   • The rock climber forgot to bring his rope and pitons; however, he remembered to bring the food.

Some people think a word like *however* should always have a semicolon before it. No—the word *however* can move from the beginning of the independent clause to the middle or end of it. The semicolon still stays between the independent clauses—thus separating similar grammatical units:

- The rock climber forgot to bring his rope and pitons; he remembered, however, to bring the food.

2. Use a semicolon to separate items in series if any item in the series has commas in it.

Here's a sentence with incorrect punctuation—notice the confusion:

- *Confusing:* Many stars from the carnival were there: the ringmaster, Harpo and Groucho, the clowns, Feline, the lion tamer, Ursula, the bear, and, fortunately, Zorro, the bear tamer.

Now let's add semicolons—notice how much easier the sentence is to understand:

- *Correct:* Many stars from the carnival were there: the ringmaster; Harpo and Groucho, the clowns; Feline, the lion tamer; Ursula, the bear; and, fortunately, Zorro, the bear tamer.

But bullets would be better, wouldn't they?

✧   ✧   ✧

Experiment with these marks and with those you already know how to use: parentheses, question marks, and italicizing for emphasis. The results will be dramatic.

MORE ABOUT
ORGANIZATION

CHAPTER 9

Blueprint

Bottom line

Tell your readers, up front, the structure of your document.

This chapter will cover three topics:

- What is a blueprint?

- Do you always need a blueprint?

- How can you write a good blueprint?

What is a blueprint?

A blueprint is simply a brief outline of what you'll cover. Here's an example:

> From my point of view, we may classify risks as:
>
> - noncommercial
>
> - political
>
> - financial
>
> Let's look more closely at these.

As a reader, you now know the structure of the document you've just begun to read: you know it has three parts, you know what they are, and you know the order they should appear in.

As a writer, you usually want your reader to be comfortable with the structure of your document. That way, your reader can spend more energy concentrating on its content.

A blueprint is especially important for documents longer than a page or so. Think of your document as a trip for your reader. The blueprint is like a road map—saying what various stops you're going to make along the way: "First, we'll look at noncommercial risks, then move on to political risks, and finally end with financial risks."

Tip

Use a heading for each section of your document that you've blueprinted. For example, you could have a heading for your discussion of each of the three risks: noncommercial, political, and financial. The headings then become like road signs for your reader's "trip."

Let's look at another blueprint, this from *Consumer Reports*, telling us how to buy a new car:

> Before you think of shopping for a car, do your homework. Approach your car-shopping methodically, in the following sequence:
>
> - Narrow your choices of cars and equipment.
> - Find out what the dealer paid the factory for the car.
> - Shop more than one dealer.
> - Keep the transaction as simple and straightforward as possible.
>
> Let's examine each step in detail.

As a reader, you now know, without guessing, the structure of the document you've just begun to read.

Do you always need a blueprint?

No. If your document is short, telling its structure may seem too mechanical.

Another time a blueprint may seem too mechanical is when your document has many parts. Suppose, for example, it has nine sections. Readers normally don't want to read through a list of the nine topics you're going to cover. On the other hand, a document with nine sections can get confusing, can't it?

So I suggest using an implied blueprint: "I'll cover the nine issues in the case, starting with the most important one." Your reader now knows the structure of your document. You've given the number of "stops" on the trip but not the lengthy list of their names.

And what if you can't give a blueprint of your document? That means you probably haven't organized it into clear blocks of information. Very occasionally that's okay for a document. Most times, though, busy readers will become confused and start skimming.

How can you write a good blueprint?

Here are some tips for writing good blueprints:

- Consider highlighting (such as using bullets) to emphasize the blueprint list.

- Put a sentence after the blueprint telling your readers you're going to say more about each item ("Let's examine each step in detail"). That way your readers know they've read not just a list—but a list of the topics you're about to elaborate on.

- Be sure that the headings in the body of your document match the key words in your blueprint. For example, the first heading in the *Consumer Reports* article on buying a car is "Narrow Your Choices." The heading helps reinforce the structure of the document.

❖   ❖   ❖

As I mentioned in Chapter 5, this may all seem mechanical. But when we're reading complex information, a clear structure is a huge benefit. The blueprint helps your reader understand that structure.

CHAPTER 10

Executive summary

Bottom line

For longer documents, summarize up front—including your bottom line.

An executive summary is like an "elevator briefing." Here's what I mean: Suppose you get on an elevator with your boss, who asks, "How's your project going?" You need to finish your answer by the time you get to the fourth floor. What would you say?

You'd probably give a quick, bottom-line summary. And what's effective for a busy person on an elevator is also effective for a busy person sitting at a desk. An executive summary, then, is a quick, bottom-line summary. The difference from an elevator briefing is that the executive summary is in writing.

An executive summary normally is at the beginning of a document. And it's normally short.

In this chapter, let's consider these questions:

- Who reads an executive summary?
- How long should an executive summary be?
- Is there a structure for an executive summary?
- What are some cautions?

73

Who reads an executive summary?

The answer seems obvious: executives, of course. That's true—but not the whole story.

The main reason for an executive summary is often to let a busy executive, usually a highly placed boss, read the summary instead of the document itself. If the executive summary is good, the executive can learn all the important bottom-line information up front.

However, there are other important audiences:

- *Other people who are too busy to read the document.* The top boss may not be the only one who doesn't have time for the entire document but still needs the quick bottom line. Staff members, for example, may have such a need.

- *People wondering if they ought to read the document.* Without an executive summary, the only way to know if a document is relevant is to read it. But with a well-designed executive summary, the decision becomes much easier.

- *People who will read the entire document anyway.* Let's face it: *all* of us appreciate an executive summary. If we have to read the entire document anyway, the executive summary provides context—all the bottom-line information right there at the beginning.

How long should an executive summary be?

The traditional answer is "one page." However, I've seen good ones that are three pages long (for 40-page documents). And I've seen other good ones that are only a paragraph.

Is there a general structure for an executive summary?

I think so:

- Executive summaries should usually begin with the bottom line. That three-page executive summary I just mentioned had the bottom line up front. In a way, the beginning was like a summary within a summary—a good way to begin. What if the bottom line doesn't make sense at the very beginning? Then I'd give the *minimum* background necessary to understand the bottom line first—followed immediately by the bottom line. Normally a sentence or two of background is enough.

- The middle part of the summary should be "skimmable." That is, it should probably have headings and bullets. Key illustrations are also entirely appropriate.

- The end of the summary should explain the structure of the main report to the reader. Think of this as a blueprint of what's to follow.

Now let's look at an executive summary. This is the summary of a report to the head of a chain of shoe stores, urging a particular way for the stores to buy shoes.

Main recommendation
This report recommends we buy most of our shoes from wholesalers during visits to the wholesalers' warehouses.

The problem
Now we buy shoes from the following sources:

- catalogs
- sales calls
- shows
- visits to wholesalers

The result? Too often we have shoes cluttering our store—shoes in strange colors, styles, and sizes that we have trouble selling. Worse, we often don't have the right colors, styles, and sizes to make sales.

That's why I recommend visiting wholesalers. That way, we can see the actual colors and styles we purchase, and we can check for quality and fit. Then we won't be stuck with shoes we can't sell.

What this report covers
In this report, I discuss the advantages and disadvantages of each way we buy shoes. And then I explain why the last way—visits to wholesalers—is better than each of the other ways.

You can see how valuable this summary would be to a reader about to read the lengthy report.

Tip

Spend lots of time getting the words just right in your executive summary. Remember that more people probably read the executive summary than any other part of a report. The summary should show the <u>most</u> crafting—not the least.

What are some cautions?

Too often, writers forget the purpose of an executive summary—something to read *instead of* the entire report. As a result, two problems sometimes occur.

Sometimes the summary doesn't give the bottom line. The summary to the head of the shoe stores *does* give it: buy from wholesalers. However, what if the summary said only something like this?

This report recommends ways to buy our shoes. These are the sources the report considers:

- catalogs
- sales calls
- shows
- visits to wholesalers

The report examines each of these in detail and then makes a recommendation.

You can see that this version simply announces the topic; it doesn't give the recommendation (buy from wholesalers). Readers of executive summaries *especially* want the recommendation—that's often the main reason they're looking at the report.

A second problem with executive summaries is that they may use unfamiliar jargon. Often reports—especially technical ones—take care to define new terms before they use those terms later in the report. Poor executive summaries sometimes include those same terms—without defining them.

There's a great temptation to use the undefined terminology in the summary because defining it might take up valuable space. That's true, but the answer is not to use the unfamiliar terminology anyway. The answer is to find plain English equivalents so you can talk in general terms.

For example, suppose I'm writing a report on types of writing needs for people in business. I wouldn't use the term *syntactic fluency* in the executive summary, even though that term might be crucial in the report, itself. Instead, for the summary, I'd use a plain English paraphrase: "help people learn to vary their sentence structure." I'll wait to use the technical term until I've defined it in the report, itself.

And a third problem with executive summaries is that inexperienced writers sometimes create them by cutting and pasting sentences and paragraphs from the report. The resulting summaries tend to be fragmented and incoherent.

✣   ✣   ✣

Now on to some ways to improve layout—which computers have made not only possible, but fun!

MORE ABOUT
LAYOUT

CHAPTER 11

Typefaces

Bottom line

Choose your typefaces carefully. The right ones can mean whether your readers pick up your document in the first place.

We have incredible power over the look of our documents—more power than entire print shops of a decade ago. The trick is to use that power effectively for conveying the message. The goal of this chapter is to show you how.

These are my suggestions:

- Prefer serif type for your main text.

- Prefer sans serif type for most headings.

- Choose your type size carefully.

- Be careful with full justification.

- Restrict bold to titles and headings.

- Use italics to emphasize text within paragraphs.

After explaining these suggestions, I'll finish with some sample typefaces for you to compare.

Prefer serif type for your main text

There are many ways to classify typefaces, but the most common is whether or not they have serifs. Can you see the difference between the letters in the left and right columns?

The letters on the left have small lines at the ends of the strokes. Those are "serifs." The letters on the right don't have those small lines and are "sans serif." (*Sans* is French for "without.")

I recommend serif type for your main text (basically, the text for your paragraphs—excluding titles, headings, etc.).

Why? Simply because that's what we're used to. In the United States, an overwhelming number of documents use serif typefaces for the main text. Just check the newspapers, magazines, and books you read. You'll see serif almost all the time except for headings and titles and other occasional uses.

So using serif type for your main text is a standard. That doesn't mean that's the right way to do things—just the common way. Professionals often do creative and effective things that violate standards.

So can you.

Here are some common serif typefaces (all 12-point type):

New Baskerville:	abcdefghijklmnop
New Century Schoolbook:	abcdefghijklmnop
Palatino:	abcdefghijklmnop
Times New Roman:	abcdefghijklmnop

Prefer sans serif type for most headings

Sans serif type makes a nice heading—it contrasts with the serif type in your main text. Because of that contrast, sans serif type also works nicely for block quotations, indented examples, captions, and sidebars.

Here are some common sans serif typefaces (all 12-point type):

Arial:	abcdefghijklmnop
Avant Garde:	abcdefghijklmnop
Helvetica:	abcdefghijklmnop
Optima:	abcdefghijklmnop

If you're wondering why Avant Garde looks big and Optima looks small—yet both are in 12-point type—the next section explains why.

Choose your type size carefully

When I ask people what type size is appropriate for the main text in their business writing, almost all say, immediately, "12 point." A better answer, though, is, "It depends." And it depends on these three things:

- How long are your lines?
- How wide is your type?
- How tall are the basic lower case letters?

How long are your lines?

Have you ever wondered why we can read small type fairly easily in a newspaper but not in a standard business letter? That's because the length of the line on a page is almost as important as the size of the type. We can read 10-point type in a newspaper column that's two inches wide. However, if we tried that in a column six inches wide, we'd be squinting.

Most business writing is in a single column on an 8½ by 11 inch sheet of paper. With normal margins, the length of your line will be about six inches or so. For that length, you'll probably want to use a type size that's 12 or 12½ or 13 points. To decide which, you need to consider the next two topics.

How wide is your type?

Have you ever noticed that 12-point type sometimes looks smaller than at other times? Actually, in a way, it *is* smaller! That's because typesetters measure the size of type only by its *height*, not by its width, yet both affect how large or small the type appears to us. Typesetters measure the size of type in points (1/72 inch):

 *point size*

When we say a type size is 12 points, we essentially mean
that the vertical distance from the top of the tallest character to the bottom of the lowest is 12 points.

But some typefaces have letters that are *wide*—which point
size doesn't measure. As a result, these typefaces look big
for their point size. Other typefaces are narrow—and look
small for their point size.

You can see that effect when you look at the alphabet in
two different typefaces. Notice that the sample of Times
New Roman takes less space across the page than New
Baskerville does:

> Times New Roman: abcdefghijklmnopqrstuvwxyz
> New Baskerville: abcdefghijklmnopqrstuvwxyz

Both samples are in 12-point type, but Times New Roman
is more narrow—or *compressed*—than is New Baskerville.
The difference may seem slight, but if you print an entire
page of each typeface, you'll instantly see the differences:

- The compressed typeface—Times New Roman—seems
  smaller.

- The compressed typeface also seems to make the page
  darker and sometimes more cluttered.

Tip

> *To find out how compressed or expanded your typefaces
> are, simply do what I just did: type the entire alphabet for
> several typefaces and compare them.*

With a compressed typeface, then, I recommend that you
use 12½ or 13 points. But before you make your decision,
you need to consider the final topic: the height of the
lower case letters.

How tall are the basic lower case letters?

As I just discussed, one reason type can look small is that it is compressed. Another reason is that the basic lower case letters may be short. For the sake of explanation, let's say that basic lower case letters include:

- letters not having ascenders or descenders, like *a, c, o,* and *x,* to name a few

- the parts of letters—like *b, d, p*—not including the ascenders and descenders (just the bowls of the *b,* the *d,* and the *p,* for example)

Within a particular typeface, all basic lower case letters are about the same height. But the basic lower case letters in one typeface may be much taller or shorter than those in another typeface.

For example, believe it or not, both of these next examples are the same overall point size—as the lines across the top and bottom show:

Remember that type size is the *height* of an entire typeface, essentially from the top of the highest character to the bottom of the lowest one.

Some typefaces, like Cochin, have really long ascenders and descenders:

As a result, there's not much height left for the basic lower case letters—and they get squeezed into a small vertical space. They look smaller and are harder to read in small point sizes.

On the other hand, some typefaces, like Avant Garde, have really short ascenders and descenders:

short ascender — ... — *plenty of room for basic lower case letters*

short descender —

As a result, there's plenty of height left for the basic lower case letters—and the typeface is more readable at smaller sizes.

So now let's put this discussion of typefaces all together with some recommendations (there are samples of all these typefaces at the end of the chapter):

- *Times New Roman.* This serif typeface looks small on the page in 12-point type because the typeface is compressed. I prefer 13-point type but 12½ may suffice.

- *New Baskerville, New Century Schoolbook, and Palatino.* These serif typefaces look all right in 12-point type; however, I lean toward 12½ for New Baskerville and Palatino. They're a little more compressed than New Century Schoolbook.

- *Arial and Helvetica.* These sans serif typefaces make excellent headings. They both are not very compressed and have large lower case letters. As a result, they can be in bold type without the letters filling in. (You've probably seen letters like *o* and *d* and *p* in boldface with type filling into the middle.)

- *Avant Garde.* This is big—really big—for its point size. It's a very expanded sans serif typeface and has large lower case letters. As a result, Avant Garde works well in bold type, remaining readable in small sizes.

Be careful with full justification

Much of the time full justification is appropriate but not always. Here's the explanation.

There are three types of justification:

- *Full justification.* Both left and right margins are even.

- *Left justification.* Only the left margin is even; the right is ragged.

- *Right justification.* Only the right margin is even; the left is ragged.

Here is a sample of each:

Fully justified. This paragraph is fully justified. This paragraph is fully justified. This paragraph is fully justified. This paragraph is fully justified. This paragraph is fully justified. This paragraph is fully justified.

Left justified. This paragraph is left justified. This paragraph is left justified. This paragraph is left justified. This paragraph is left justified. This paragraph is left justified. This paragraph is left justified.

Right justified. This paragraph is right justified. This paragraph is right justified. This paragraph is right justified. This paragraph is right justified. This paragraph is right justified. This paragraph is right justified.

With most typefaces, either full justification or left justification is fine. Right justification is for special effects. The title on a cover page, for example, sometimes looks nice with right justification.

You want to avoid full justification with primarily one typeface: Courier. With Courier (and some of its relatives), full justification tends to leave uneven gaps between some of the words. I'm sure you've seen the problem. The uneven spacing makes the text harder to read.

The problem is that Courier is a monospaced typeface. Courier was an extremely popular choice of typewriter ball for the old IBM Selectric typewriter. Like most typewriter typefaces, each letter and number took up the *same width* on the page (hence, *mono*spaced):

ilmw

Notice that the normally narrow letters—*i* and *l*—are pretty wide. And the normally wide letters—*m* and *w*—are pretty narrow. Each character in Courier has the same width. As a result, there are few spacing tools for the printer to play with to make fully justified lines. If a big word won't quite fit at the end of the line, it moves to the next line. That leaves big spaces in the line above.

Tip

Avoid Courier unless you have a really good reason to use it. Courier looks like an old-fashioned typewriter did it. I've taken many straw polls, and clear majorities are tired of Courier.

Proportional typefaces, on the other hand, have a much easier time with full justification. Here's a sample of a proportional typeface:

ilmw

Notice that the *i* and *l* are much narrower than the *m* and *w*. Because the characters have varying widths (and the space character can vary), proportional typefaces have more "tools" to stop the gaps.

So *avoid* full justification with Courier and any other monospaced typefaces you may have. But with proportional typefaces—Times New Roman, Palatino, and all the others we've talked about in this chapter—full justification and left justification both work well.

Restrict bold to titles and headings

Bold and *italics* both emphasize your words:

- Bold emphasizes a lot. It **stands out** from several feet away. That can be good or bad. It works great for headings. It can distract needlessly when you use it to emphasize words in paragraphs (as here).

- Italics emphasizes a little. It *stands out* when you're actually reading the words—not from several feet away.

I recommend that you use bold for your title and most of your headings and seldom anyplace else.

Use italics to emphasize text within paragraphs

If you've used bold for the major elements of your document, italics then works nicely for items of lesser emphasis—especially for words *within* paragraphs. Italics gives more emphasis than normal upright text but less emphasis than bold. It emphasizes when you need to without needlessly distracting your reader.

Sample typefaces

Here are samples of most of the typefaces we've talked about in the chapter. Look closely at how many words are on the first line of each sample. You'll see, for example, that Courier is really expanded and Times New Roman is really compressed. Also notice the overall look of the typeface and whether it appeals to you.

Times New Roman

This is a sample of 12-point type to help you compare typefaces. This is a sample of 12-point type to help you compare typefaces. This is a sample of 12-point type to help you compare typefaces.

Courier

```
This is a sample of 12-point type to
help you compare typefaces. This is a
sample of 12-point type to help you
compare typefaces. This is a sample of
12-point type to help you compare
typefaces
```

New Baskerville

This is a sample of 12-point type to help you compare typefaces. This is a sample of 12-point type to help you compare typefaces. This is a sample of 12-point type to help you compare typefaces.

   (This is the typeface for the main text in this book.)

New Century Schoolbook

This is a sample of 12-point type to help you compare typefaces. This is a sample of 12-point type to help you compare typefaces. This is a sample of 12-point type to help you compare typefaces.

Palatino

This is a sample of 12-point type to help you compare typefaces. This is a sample of 12-point type to help you compare typefaces. This is a sample of 12-point type to help you compare typefaces.

Arial

This is a sample of 12-point type to help you compare typefaces. This is a sample of 12-point type to help you compare typefaces. This is a sample of 12-point type to help you compare typefaces.

Avant Garde

This is a sample of 12-point type to help you compare typefaces. This is a sample of 12-point type to help you compare typefaces. This is a sample of 12-point type to help you compare typefaces.

(This is the typeface for most headings in this book.)

Optima

This is a sample of 12-point type to help you compare typefaces. This is a sample of 12-point type to help you compare typefaces. This is a sample of 12-point type to help you compare typefaces.

Tip

> *Print a full page of one of your typical documents in several typefaces and sizes. Compare them. You'll probably have a clear preference right away.*

❖   ❖   ❖

As you've seen, there are some important things to know about typefaces, but there are few rights and wrongs. Look at the wonderful ways professionals use type in books and magazines. Then start experimenting until you get the look you like.

CHAPTER 12

Headings

Bottom line

A good layout for headings can help your readers <u>see</u> the structure of your writing; a bad layout may only confuse them. Headings are a key that you can use in almost every document.

Good headings can make a terrific difference in most of your documents! At a glance, your reader can see that your documents *look* organized.

Headings also help show where the parts of your documents begin and end. Headings make nice reference points when your reader is trying to find something again. And they help you organize your thoughts in the first place.

But just having headings isn't good enough. Too often, people use confusing layouts for headings. This chapter will cover some fundamentals that will help your headings work for your readers.

Here's a summary of my tips for headings:

- Put more space above a heading than below it.
- Make sub-headings clearly subordinate to your main headings.
- Use at least two of each kind of heading.

At the end, I'll show you some sample headings.

Put more space above a heading than below it

A heading can do more than signal a new topic. It can also help group all the text for that topic.

The example on the left doesn't; the one on the right does:

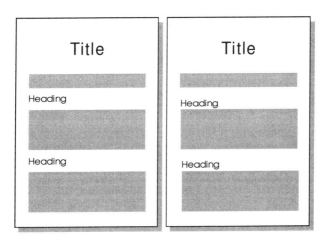

See the difference? The headings in the left sample float between sections; the headings on the right are clearly attached to something—the blocks of information that they label.

Make sub-headings clearly subordinate to your main headings

Headings label blocks of information. Sometimes you may have subdivided your blocks into parts and want to label them, too. So you need headings *and* sub-headings.

Here is an illustration:

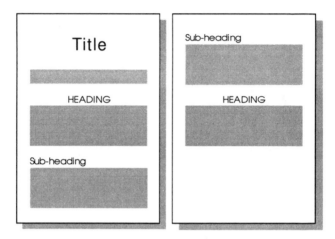

What you don't want to do, however, is to have headings that mislead your reader. Notice that the first heading looks subordinate to the next one, the sub-heading:

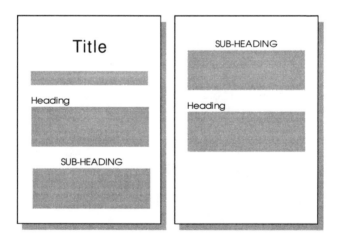

The sub-heading, which is upper case and centered, looks more important than the main heading, doesn't it? When you design your headings, you need to be sure they work with the priority your readers have learned—perhaps unconsciously—from having read thousands and thousands of pages of printed material. So when you choose the styles you want for your headings, you have to be careful to observe this hierarchy of importance:

- Upper case has priority over lower case:

THIS IS A HEADING / This is a heading

That is, if we see a heading that's all upper case, we'll probably figure that it labels a higher level section than a heading that's mainly lower case.

- Bold has priority over italics:

This is a heading / *This is a heading*

Again, we'll assume a bold heading probably labels a higher level section than a heading that's in italics. That's because bold tends to stand out more.

- Sans serif has priority over serif (if your main text is serif):

This is a heading / This is a heading

We'll probably assume that a sans serif heading labels a higher level section than a heading using the same serif typeface as the main text.

- A large type size has priority over a small type size:

This is a heading / This is a heading

Also:

- More space above and below a heading has priority over less.

- Centered has priority over starting on the left margin.

- A line from margin to margin underneath a heading gives priority over a heading without one.

Use at least two of each kind of heading

When readers see a heading, they automatically think—as a result of their experience—that they're seeing the first of several sections like that. In other words, they'd be surprised to find out that your document looks like this:

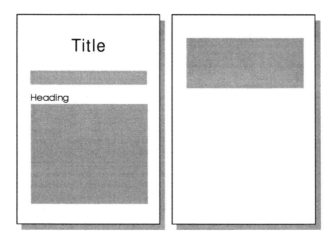

But this next one works with your reader's expectations:

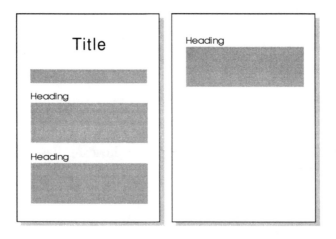

Sample headings

There is a nearly limitless number of ways to make headings. This section shows you just a few samples. In each case, notice that the sub-heading is subordinate to the main heading in at least *two* ways.

That is, if the main heading is upper case and centered, the sub-heading shouldn't be the same except that it starts on the left margin. The main heading and sub-heading would look too similar. When readers turn to a page with only one heading, they might not remember if it's your main heading or your sub-heading.

But if your sub-headings are different in at least two ways, your readers are more likely to immediately tell whether a single heading on a page is the main one or the subordinate one. For example, there are three differences between the main and sub-headings in this example. Can you spot them?

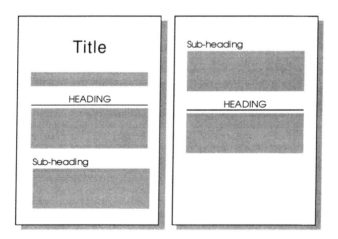

Here are the three differences—each giving priority to the main heading over the layout of the sub-heading:

- The main heading has a line under it from margin to margin.
- The main heading is centered.
- The main heading is all upper case.

Now let's look at another way to make headings:

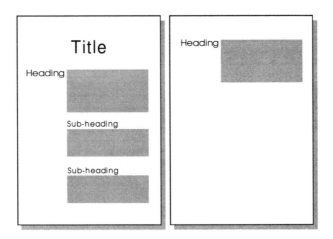

These main headings—the ones on the left margin—are "hanging headings."

They're quite common today for reports because of the white space they add. The page seems open and accessible, doesn't it?

Some people think that hanging headings waste space and make a document longer. Actually, though, the document gets only a little longer. That's because you can use a smaller type size for your main text.

Remember that the length of your line is important in choosing a type size. Because the hanging heading reduces the length of your line of main text, a smaller size works fine.

How much smaller? A point or so.

Tip

Use headings on most documents longer than about half a page. Even short documents benefit markedly from headings.

There can be a problem with hanging headings, though: you have to know how to work with two columns on your computer—one column for your headings, another for your text.

If you're not comfortable working with columns, a similar style of headings is easy to do:

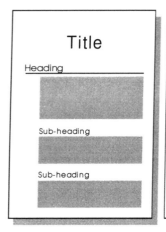

With this style, you simply indent your text more than you indent your main headings.

✢   ✢   ✢

There are many, many more ways to make headings. Look around, experiment, and find the ones that give the look you want for your document.

CHAPTER 13

Bullets

Bottom line

*As with headings, a good layout for bullets can help your readers
<u>see</u> the structure of your writing; a bad layout may only confuse
them.*

As you can tell, I consider the bullet a magical device, a
wonderful way to help untangle ideas and show readers
the organization within paragraphs.

In Chapter 4, we looked at bulleted *lists*. This chapter looks
at bulleted *paragraphs* and then discusses ways to add polish to the way you present both bulleted lists and bulleted
paragraphs.

Let's start with the bulleted paragraph.

What is a bulleted paragraph?

You needn't feel that bullets show only single sentences,
like this:

> After 3 months of examining your records for the past
> year, we have found the following:
>
> - Your marketing division is systematically hiding its
>   losses each month—totaling $300,000 for the past 6
>   months alone.

- The division manager and her assistant appear to be the only people involved.

- There were no other major discrepancies.

You can also have short paragraphs as bullets:

After 3 months of examining your records for the past year, we have found the following:

- Your marketing division is systematically hiding its losses each month—totaling $300,000 for the past 6 months alone. This may have been taking place for years—we did not have access to your records before last June.

- The division manager and her assistant appear to be the only people involved now. Some former employees may have been involved, however. For example, the former budget clerk just bought a Mercedes sports car and has moved to Hawaii. Perhaps he was involved, too.

Why use bulleted paragraphs? The usual answer: they show your reader the organization of your document. Notice that normal paragraphing doesn't do that:

After 3 months of examining your records for the past year, we have found the following:

Your marketing division is systematically hiding its losses each month—totaling $300,000 for the past 6 months alone. This may have been taking place for years—we did not have access to your records before last June.

The division manager and her assistant appear to be the only people involved now. Some former employees may have been involved, however. For example, the former budget clerk just bought a Mercedes sports car and has moved to Hawaii. Perhaps he was involved, too.

All three of those paragraphs look the same, as though they're at the same level of subordination. Actually, as we've seen, the second and third paragraphs are subordinate to the first. Bulleted paragraphs show that relationship better.

What symbol should you use for bullets?

There isn't just one symbol for bullets. Here are some perfectly acceptable ways for making the bullet symbol:

- This is the traditional symbol.

- This bullet is common, too. It echoes the rectangular shapes on many pages (paragraphs, illustrations, etc.). You may need to reduce its point size to make it look right.

- This bullet adds flair. Again, you may need to reduce its point size.

- This is what people often use when they can't figure out how to get the other symbols out of their computers.

These ways all work fine, but you wouldn't want to use all of them in the same list, as I've done here.

By the way, if you check newspapers and magazines, you can find many different bullet symbols: squiggles, check marks, happy faces, graphic art (drawings of small pencils, for example), and so forth. These have their places, too, depending on the tone you want to set.

What spacing should you use
for bulleted lists and paragraphs?

The reason for using bulleted lists and paragraphs is to isolate and group information, so you want to use plenty of white space. Here's a bulleted list that does just about everything wrong:

> After 3 months of examining your records for the past year, we have found the following:
> •Your marketing division is systematically hiding its losses each month—totaling $300,000 for the past 6 months alone.
> •The division manager and her assistant appear be the only people involved.
> •There were no other major discrepancies.
> The attached report discusses these three findings.

Not effective, is it? I suggest double spacing between bulleted items (especially if any one of them is more than a line long). Here are some other tips on spacing:

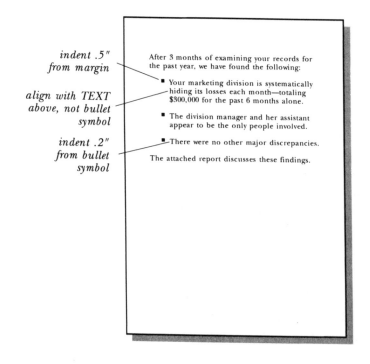

indent .5"
from margin

align with TEXT
above, not bullet
symbol

indent .2"
from bullet
symbol

After 3 months of examining your records for the past year, we have found the following:

■ Your marketing division is systematically hiding its losses each month—totaling $300,000 for the past 6 months alone.

■ The division manager and her assistant appear to be the only people involved.

■There were no other major discrepancies.

The attached report discusses these findings.

This spacing will help you "show off" your list so it can gain the attention it deserves.

How should you punctuate bulleted lists?

When you're using bulleted *paragraphs,* you don't have to worry about using special punctuation—just punctuate normally.

However, when you're using bulleted *lists,* you may wonder whether to start with a capital letter and whether to put a period at the end. After all, some lists are only words or phrases.

There are two common methods: the traditional method and the contemporary method (which I learned from Dr. Ginny Redish).

The traditional method—still quite popular—simply keeps the punctuation the list would have if it were part of a normal paragraph. Here's a list that's part of a normal paragraph—it's not bulleted yet:

> The order was late on April 15, late on April 16, and on time on April 17.

The traditional method would keep that same punctuation, pretending the list is still part of a regular sentence:

> The order was:
>
> - late on April 15,
>
> - late on April 16, and
>
> - on time on April 17.

The contemporary method—gaining popularity—stops the pretense that there's a sentence and gets rid of the commas, the period, and the word *and*:

The order was:

- late on April 15

- late on April 16

- on time on April 17

Where's the period to end the sentence? I don't know. There simply isn't one. But readers are more likely to notice a period *there* than a period *missing*. The contemporary method places more importance on each item in the list having the same appearance than on pretending the list is still a "sentence."

So here's how the contemporary method handles punctuation and capitalization:

- If the bulleted item is a sentence, make it look like one (that is, start with a capital letter and put a period at the end).

- If the bulleted item is *not* a sentence, don't. That is, don't start with a capital letter and don't put any punctuation at the end.

Let's look at several examples. You've seen the next one before. Notice that the items in it are not sentences, so they don't begin with capital letters or end with periods:

The order was:

- late on April 15

- late on April 16

- on time on April 17

Now let's rewrite that example to make the items into sentences. Notice that they now look like sentences—with capital letters and periods:

Here's what happened to the orders:

- They were late on April 15.
- They were late on April 16.
- They were on time on April 17.

Tip

Be sure your lists are parallel. That is, lists should never have some items that are full sentences and some that aren't. Once you set up a pattern for a list, you must stick to it—all full sentences or all only phrases.

Sometimes you have items that are only phrases but then you want to add a comment or two. What do you do? Well, here's a solution involving a little rewriting:

Here's what happened:

- *April 15.* The order was 15 minutes late (arriving at 9:15).
- *April 16.* The order was 35 minutes late (arriving at 9:35).
- *April 17.* The order was on time (arriving at 8:55).

This combines the topics of the last two chapters—bullets *and* headings. They work well separately; they work well together. And both make the reader's job much easier.

Now for the final chapter on layout: graphics.

CHAPTER 14

Graphics

Bottom line

Today's writers need to get beyond paragraphs full of words.
Tables, drawings, graphs, and other illustrations are often what
readers remember most.

If you look at a page with an illustration on it, don't you look at the illustration first? And if you look at a page with nothing but paragraphs full of words, don't you wish there were an illustration there?

I imagine most of us have learned to value illustrations. There are some obvious types of illustrations. For example:

- If you want to show how your profits have increased over the past five years, use a line graph or bar chart.

- If you're talking about the gill structure of an obscure tropical fish, use a drawing.

- If you want to show the latest Parisian design for an evening gown, show a photograph.

Those are all useful. They'll have impact. And your readers will remember them.

These types of graphics are all good, but you already know about them. This chapter talks about some other techniques. Whenever you find yourself struggling to describe something in paragraphs full of words, maybe one of these can help:

- using a creative layout for your words
- using a highlighted figure
- including the object itself
- using a diagram

Using a creative layout for your words

Sometimes you can creatively place your words on the page. The effect is to draw your reader to that information.

For example, a simple table can clearly show your logic. Here's one showing options for producing a large, complex report:

Option	Advantages	Disadvantages
Do it manually.	No computer costs.	Takes forever.
Give everybody a big, powerful, expensive computer to process the data.	People get reports more quickly.	High cost of computers.
Give everybody a less powerful, cheaper computer AND one big, powerful, expensive computer for the entire group.	People get reports more quickly AND costs are cheaper.	None.

This logic table makes the writer's point much more quickly than the same ideas in a few paragraphs.

Here's another example of a creative way to present words. In this case, a woman is describing her position as a "floater" in a law office's secretarial pool:

F flexibility. This is the key to being effective. I sit at a secretary's station surrounded by *that* person's equipment and *that* person's organization of files. My job is to familiarize myself with these as quickly as possible.

L legal secretarial skills. I must be able to type quickly (at least 80 wpm), take shorthand, and use the computer network efficiently.

O other duties as assigned. I have performed such duties as notarizing documents, inventorying supplies, boxing files for storage, and logging in billing information.

A ability to work every machine. I must be able to use the many different computers as well as more than one kind of copier, fax machine, transcriber, etc.

T telephone savvy. For those attorneys who do not answer their telephone lines, I have to know when it is appropriate to interrupt to announce an incoming call.

E editing skills. Much of my work involves correcting an attorney's product.

R receptionist skills. On rare occasions, I sit in for one of our four receptionists. I dislike this job the most. If I hear they are looking for someone to cover the phones, I hide out in the bathroom!

Using a highlighted example

The highlighted example is another way to present words in a more visual way. Here's the illustration that accompanied a description of "National Stock Number":

Digits 1 - 4:
Federal Stock Class

Digits 5 - 13:
National Item Identification Number

1006 - 00 - 123 - 4567

country code   serial number

The writer then explained each part of the number and gave an example. The labels at the bottom—"country code" and "serial number"—are "callouts." They point to information on an illustration and are extremely useful.

Including the object itself

I once read a memo discussing fiber optics. The author taped a sample on the first page. Believe me, one strand took up little space. Perhaps there are times you're describing something that is small and cheap enough to attach.

Using a diagram

A diagram is a good way to describe something with several components. In this, the writer showed the hidden costs that businesses recover in order to be profitable:

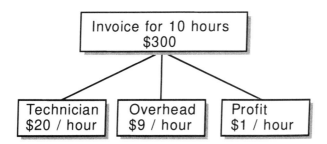

Tip

Once you write a longer document, consciously look it over for places to add graphics (or to replace paragraphs with graphics).

And here's another one showing the hiring process for a large organization (as you review it, imagine trying to say the same thing in paragraphs full of words):

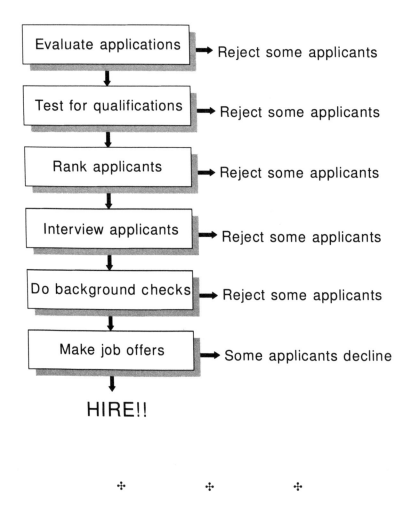

Images like these take a little creativity, but they make a world of difference for your readers.

FINAL WORDS
ON WRITING

CHAPTER 15

The writing process

Bottom line

A good writing process makes getting words on the page easier.

So far this book has been totally concerned with the *product* of your writing: your document should have a clear style, start with the bottom line, and use good layout.

This chapter is about the *process* of writing. It shows how you can get words on paper easily.

What's a good writing process?

Is this the writing process you learned?

Prewriting
1. Think hard.
2. Write an outline.

Writing
1. Follow your outline.
2. Write quickly without worrying about revisions.

Rewriting
1. Make sure you followed your outline.
2. Fix any errors.

Well, there's surely some truth there, but there are some half-truths, too.

The role of the outline

What's the role of an outline? Should you have one? Most business people I speak with confess: they rarely use an outline, and they virtually never use a formal outline (you know—I, A, B, II, A, B).

Outlines do have advantages, though. It's always helpful to know where you're going before you start. But sometimes writers simply aren't quite sure where they're going *until* they write; that is, as they struggle to put thoughts into those elusive things called words, learning takes place: new ideas emerge and old ideas take new shape. We've all had that experience.

In other words, sometimes we have trouble writing an effective outline at the beginning of the writing process. Starting "cold" seems to produce either bad outlines or, worse, only a blank piece of paper and a deep sense of guilt.

For something under a page or so, don't worry about an outline at all. It probably isn't necessary. For something longer—even just slightly longer—an outline may be helpful. Here's what I recommend:

- If you have excellent understanding of your content at the start, try making an outline. Don't worry about those Roman numerals—just jot something down. You may want to jot down only main headings.

- If you're a little unsure of your content, try jotting down several ideas in the order you think you should cover them. Then start writing. After writing two or three paragraphs, you'll probably warm up; that is, your mind will be focused on your material—more saturated with the information you want to cover. So reassess your outline and redo it if necessary—this time perhaps in a little more detail.

- If you're embarking on a long writing project or one involving other writers, work hard to get a good— even formal—outline on paper before you begin.

A "recursive" process

Researchers today believe that most writing doesn't take place in a linear order: first prewriting, then writing, then rewriting. Rather, there's lots of moving back and forth. Researchers call that "recursiveness."

But . . . a linear draft

Even though your writing process may be recursive, your draft should usually be linear. That is, you should start at the beginning and work your way straight through. The other way—writing part 2 before part 1, for example—can cause problems.

Here's why. If you have a good organization, your reader will read the document in order: page 1, then page 2, then page 3. So for you to write page 3, you need to know what the reader has already seen on pages 1 and 2. It's amazing how often good writing refers to earlier material—or depends on it.

The final version of a good document is like a tapestry—all threads are important to the final design, and all threads are in the right place.

My own writing process

What happens on a typical writing project—something two or three pages long? Or even book length? What would be a good way to write that document?

We all have our special techniques, but here's what normally happens when I write:

1. I fool myself into believing I'm actually ready to write, so I start in.

2. I get stuck.

3. I then jot down a quick list of the main points I want to cover. If I can think of any subpoints, I put them in, too.

4. I arrange those points in the best order.

5. I start writing again.

6. If I find that I'm not following my original outline, I don't worry: my ideas while I'm actually writing are probably much better than my ideas beforehand.

7. I rarely get stuck again, but if I do, I re-outline (briefly).

8. I write quickly, with no thought for typos or other errors.

9. But I stop *immediately* if the content or organization isn't working. After all, what comes before is crucial to what comes after, so I must get the content and organization right. Otherwise, I'm wasting my time because I know I'll have to rewrite significantly.

10. When I finish writing, I read and revise immediately.

11. I then set the writing aside for awhile—even a few minutes helps disconnect my mind from the particular words on the paper.

12. Then I reread and revise, looking not just for errors but for the important matters this book covers (style, organization, and layout). Throughout, I ask these questions: "Will my reader understand?" and "Have I made my points the best way possible?"

13. Then I show the writing to someone else for feedback. I try to "lean toward" their suggestions rather than away from them. But I realize that I am the one

most responsible for the content *and* the most en-
gaged with it, so I take "my" advice before theirs.

14. I watch reruns of *Cheers* on television.

Frankly, I follow that process much of the time I write. It
works for me.

Normally I write about 5 pages or so at a sitting. Later I'll
read and revise those pages before starting a new section.
That way I'm familiar with what I've just written before
starting the writing again; also, I'll have fairly polished
pages as I move along.

What if there's not enough time?

You may not always have time to do all that. Well, the more
comfortable you are with plain English, the faster and
better you will be able to write.

Still, sometimes you can't put your writing aside. True.
And sometimes you can't show your writing to someone
else. True. But lots of times you *can*—and *should*.

Tip

*Especially for those "career" projects that come up once or
twice a year, build in the opportunity for the two feedback
steps—feedback from someone else and feedback from yourself (after getting away from the writing for awhile).*

CHAPTER 16

Supervising writers

Bottom line

Your people depend on <u>you</u> for guidance on how to write.

I know that not everybody who reads this book is a supervisor (or project leader). Some people are and many hope to be. So if you are now, this chapter is for you. And if you're not one yet? Well, this chapter is what I would tell your boss.

So . . . for supervisors—present and future: do you ever get frustrated by the writing your people do? If so, you're among the vast majority of supervisors.

Some people just don't understand the English language very well; most people, however, write "that way"—bureaucratically—because they believe they have to. They think that's the kind of writing *you want:* stilted, overly formal, passive, and "impressive."

After all, if you ever wrote in the bureaucratic style, didn't you write that way because you felt "that's what the boss wants"?

So what can you do to improve the writing of your people, to help them understand—and apply—the principles of plain English?

Here are a few tips:

Get good word processing

Make sure your people aren't still in the dark ages—get software that's up to date. Word processing from a previous generation just isn't capable of producing top-notch, professional documents.

Tell your people what you want

Remember in school when you got a paper back with red marks all over it and a comment like this: "Sentences must never begin with *and* or *but*. Don't start sentences that way in my class!" Don't you wish the teacher had told you that *before* you handed in the paper?

The same thing happens when your people write for you—if you haven't told them what you want. In fact, I suggest you tell your people in a memo that you want plain English. Tell them to write the way they talk, use pronouns, use headings, use contractions—everything. And let your memo illustrate those techniques. Then people will see the new style in action—with your signature on it.

You can use the memo time and again as you move on to new positions or as new people come to work for you. In fact, I've worked with organizations where the president's memo on writing was one of the first pieces of paper a new employee received.

Show them examples of good writing

While examples of bad writing are all over the place, examples of good writing are sometimes hard to find. But when you have such an example, you have gold. People can do an amazing job following a good example: "Oh, *that's* what you want!"

When a good example *does* cross your desk, by all means send it to all your writers—and then congratulate the person who wrote it.

When a good example does *not* ever cross your desk, then you need to take a harder step. You need to create a good example. You can do that two ways:

- You can write the example yourself.
- You can get a good writer to write one for you.

The effort, believe me, is worth it. And if you can't find a good example from your people's writing, the effort is *especially* necessary—and *especially* worth it.

Tell them when they write well for you—or badly

I know: you don't have time to give feedback to your writers. One reason you don't have time may be that you're dealing with too much of their bad writing. They'll keep turning it out, though, unless you intervene. Make an effort at least once to give detailed feedback to each writer.

Don't forget to tell them what they're doing right. If you don't give them reinforcement, they may never know what you like and may well change to something worse.

In summary . . .

Good writing is worth the effort—effort from you and from your people. Think about the struggle poor writers go through just trying to get words on paper. Think about the communication that gets lost.

The simple writing techniques in this book—on style, organization, and layout—can make all the difference to writers, readers, supervisors. Many of these techniques work nicely when you're giving a presentation, too. So if you turn the page, you can soon be on your way to giving plain English presentations!

SPEAKING
CLEARLY
&
EASILY

DESIGNING YOUR PRESENTATION

CHAPTER 17

Designing
a successful presentation

Bottom line

*Most presentations succeed or fail long before you ever stand up
to deliver them.*

Now let's turn to the second half of this book: giving
presentations in plain English. As with writing in plain
English, you should find that speaking in plain English is
clearer for your audience and easier on you, too. With a
few simple techniques, you can be on your way to being a
more effective speaker.

But for a moment, think of yourself as a member of an
audience. Have you ever sat through a presentation wondering, "What is this thing about? And when is it *ever* going
to end?"

We've all been there, haven't we? This section of the book
may not help you as a listener, but it will help you as a
speaker—so you aren't the one causing the mental grum-
bling in your audience.

You don't need to be a "born speaker" to speak well. Very
few people are. Many people who seem to be born speakers have actually gotten there through practice, more practice, and lots of experience.

But that practice isn't haphazard.

This section of the book suggests an approach for preparing your presentations, an approach I almost always use. And this approach is practical, emphasizing *how* rather than *why*:

- how to organize your presentation
- how to remember what you plan to say
- how to design visual aids
- how to design computer presentations
- how to rehearse
- how to prepare the room for your presentation
- how to handle questions and answers

And more.

What is a "business" presentation?

There is no standard business presentation. Perhaps the speaker is standing in front of a small group of people talking about work. Or selling them something. Or urging them to make a change.

Sometimes a business presentation is aimed at co-workers. Or bosses. Or subordinates. Or clients.

Sometimes it takes place in someone's office. Or in a small conference room.

Or in a hotel auditorium with hundreds of people in the audience—the speaker hooked up to a microphone, visual aids staff at the ready, lectern furnished with a glass of cold water (and the speaker's hands even colder than that).

This section of the book will help with the entire range of business presentations—because the fundamentals are the same.

What is the main message?

This is the main message: most presentations succeed or fail long before the speaker stands in front of the audience. Most presentations succeed or fail in the design stage—because a good presentation is *designed.*

By "designed" I don't mean something the graphics department does. I mean something the speaker does: the thoughtful, meticulous, purposeful preparation that helps the speaker communicate. Just as important, that preparation makes the speech far, far easier to give.

A good design, in other words, is the best way to take the pressure off. Many inexperienced speakers design a presentation that's almost bound to fail. This book will help you design one that's almost bound to succeed. Well . . . *likely* to succeed.

What, specifically, does
this section of the book cover?

This section of the book sets forth a process for designing and giving your presentation:

- *Organizing your presentation.* You'll want to begin by roughing out the general structure of your presentation—making sure it has an absolutely clear organization. If it doesn't, listeners will probably get lost, and listeners who get lost rarely find their way back. The good news is there's an organization—a pattern—that works for most business presentations.

- *Using examples.* Many presentations depend on the audience's understanding a new term—things like radiometry, type amendment, live-fire vulnerability testing, upselling, and so on. How can you be sure you communicate your key terms? The answer: examples. In fact, a well-placed example can be the difference in whether your audience even knows what you're talking about.

- *Remembering what you plan to say.* This is where most presentations get derailed. Once you've decided what to say, you need to remember it, and there are various ways to do that. Memorizing is the worst way. Well-designed visual aids are often the best.

- *Choosing visual aids.* Most business presentations rightly depend on visual aids. But when should you use an overhead projector? A flip chart? A computer presentation? Thirty-five-millimeter slides? You need to know the advantages and disadvantages of each.

- *Designing visual aids.* What should you keep in mind as you design your visual aids? How much material you put on them is extremely important. Put too little on, and you and your audience may get lost. Put too much on, and you end up simply reading aloud. Put the words in the wrong place, and people in the back of the room may not be able to see them.

- *Designing computer presentations.* These shouldn't be simply static "transparencies" projected from computers. It's important to use the computer technology fully, emphasizing meaningful activity on the screen to keep the audience's attention just where you want it at all times.

- *Using audience participation.* Most good presentations have energy flowing through them. There are ways to involve your audience even in formal speaking situations. There are also pitfalls, especially with humor, that you must be aware of.

- *Rehearsing.* Once you have prepared the content for your presentation, you need to rehearse. Rehearsing just means standing and saying the words to an empty room, right? To some extent, but there are other things you can do to make your rehearsing more efficient. Good speakers often spend a lot of time rehearsing.

- *Setting up the room.* If the room is too hot or people can't see your visual aids, you're not going to communicate well. Sometimes you don't have much control of the room, but most speakers have more control than they suspect. I'll cover what to look for in each room and how to keep problems from happening. There's a real art to this.

- *Using effective techniques of delivery.* Even with a perfect design, a presentation will surely fail if the speaker qualifies for *The Guinness Book of Records* for nervous pacing and "uh's" per second. There are important do's and don't's you should know.

- *Presenting visual aids.* The best visual aids in the world are sometimes worthless unless you know how to present them to your audience: where to stand, how to use a pointer, when to read your visual aids aloud, and when not to.

- *Handling questions and answers.* What happens when your formal presentation is over? Are you out of the woods yet? Most of the time you're not: there's a question and answer session. You can prepare for this, too. It can even be the most powerful part of your presentation.

- *Helping others speak better.* I'll finish with some advice on helping your co-workers be better speakers.

✧   ✧   ✧

Does all this sound like a lot of work? Well, "effortless" presentations are usually the product of a lot of effort. But the more you understand about presentations, the more comfortable you'll be in preparing them and—more important—in giving them.

That is, the more you feel in control, the more confident you'll be when the spotlight goes on . . . and you're in it.

So let's get started!

CHAPTER 18

Organizing your presentation

Bottom line

Business presentations should have an absolutely clear structure—the kind your audience simply will not get lost in.

When you're reading a book and get lost, you can flip back and start over. But when you're listening to a speech and get lost, well . . . there's not much you can do except sit there and consult your watch, the window, and the interior of your mind.

So when I prepare a presentation, I try to make its organization absolutely clear. As with writing, I think of a presentation as a trip, and I don't want the people in my audience to get lost. I want them to know, at the beginning, where we're going and how we'll get there.

And when the trip is under way, I want them to know exactly where we are—what town we've just passed and what's coming up.

So here's what I suggest:

- Announce your topic, define any key term, and state your bottom line.

- Then outline for your audience what the major parts of your presentation will be—that's your *blueprint*.

- And plan strong, obvious transitions throughout.

137

That said, there is no one way—no one organizational pattern—to communicate all ideas to all people. But I find this approach works most of the time. I use it when I first start to prepare. It serves me well as a starting point, and it often becomes the final organization I use.

Let's look at these suggestions more closely.

Announce your topic, define any key term, and state your bottom line

My first suggestion is to let members of your audience know the destination for their "trip." To do that, you'll need to announce your topic, define unfamiliar terms in it, and state your bottom line up front.

Announce your topic

Announcing your topic is simple: just say what you're going to talk about. You don't have to make the topic the first words out of your mouth. You might want to say a few polite sentences first—what linguists call polite noise: "Thank you, Liz, for . . ." And a little humor up front lets groups settle in and become willing to listen. But don't wait long.

To announce your topic, simply say something like:

- My purpose is to tell you how our company is doing financially.

- I'm here to talk about the promotion system for our junior staff.

- This afternoon I'm going to suggest a way to improve the quality of our proposals.

Those are so straightforward, aren't they?—clean, simple, efficient starts. The audience should begin to relax, just knowing that you actually have a clear purpose and are able to articulate it.

Define unfamiliar terms in your topic

Sometimes the topic isn't so straightforward. There may be a term in it, a necessary one, that's unfamiliar to your audience.

Here are some examples:

- Today, I'll explain the value of *type amendment.*

- I'm going to demonstrate a new *model of unit strength and cohesion.*

- I'll suggest that *fractals* can describe the behavior of two companies competing with each other.

If the topic itself has unfamiliar words in it, your audience needs to understand them immediately. Yet you've probably seen speakers go into the advantages of something like "type amendment" before defining it.

So right after you announce your topic, define any unfamiliar words in it. For example, you could explain that *type amendment* means "changing the shapes of letters to make them visually interesting or memorable."

But that still doesn't really communicate, does it?

What the audience needs now is a quick example: "Let me give you an example. In the words 'Coca-Cola,' each capital C has a unique shape—extending into a long, curvy line. That's one example of type amendment. The shape of the letter C is changed to make it visually interesting— and memorable."

Even better, use a visual aid:

To define your term, then, normally give a short plain English definition and follow with a quick example. The little time this takes is absolutely crucial for your audience.

Tip

Define only your key term in your introduction—only what your audience must know right away. Save other definitions for just when your audience needs them.

State your bottom line

Now for what audiences most want to hear up front: your bottom line. Rudolf Flesch, a pioneer in plain English writing, called that "spilling the beans." Spilling the beans is even more crucial for speaking than it is for writing. In other words, make your bottom line your top line by telling your audience, right up front, your conclusion, recommendation, or request.

For example:

- *A conclusion:* "Overall, you'll be pleased with our company's financial picture. Our profits are up 8% and our predictions are all good. Now let's look at the details."

- *A recommendation:* "The promotion system for our junior staff isn't working. I'll explain the problems and suggest we set up a promotion board to make all selections."

- *A request:* "Our division needs a color printer to help us prepare more professional proposals."

Some speakers don't like this approach, hating to give away the bottom line at the beginning. They feel audiences are more receptive who first hear *all* the facts and *all* the logical arguments and then hear the bottom line at the end.

However, I don't think their audiences would agree. From my experience, audiences that have to wait get impatient. Worse, they often get confused: all those facts and arguments simply don't mean much without the essential context of the bottom line. Imagine yourself as part of the audience: when would you want the speaker to tell you the bottom line?

So get to the point—right up front. What works best for you as a listener also works best for you as a speaker.

Tip _____

> *When you state your bottom line up front, be sure you don't give only your topic. Actually state, briefly, what you conclude, recommend, or request.*

Sometimes a presentation doesn't have a bottom line. In that case, be sure your audience isn't expecting one. That is, tell them your purpose: you're simply providing information and not asking for any action. Here's an example of a poor topic statement that may or may not have a bottom line later on:

• The topic today is our benefits program.

Is the speaker asking for more money for benefits? Or just providing information? It's impossible to tell.

This topic statement makes it clearer there's no delayed bottom line:

• This morning I'll update you on our costs last month for our benefits program.

Now the decision maker—and the rest of the audience—clearly knows the presentation's purpose. They aren't waiting for you to spring a money request on them.

So far, then, these are the first three parts of my introduction:

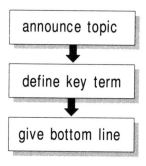

Use a blueprint

My second suggestion is to let your audience know what the subtopics are in the body of your presentation. In other words, let them know the various "places" you'll pass through on your "trip." A good way to do that is with a blueprint. A blueprint is simply a list of the parts of the body of your presentation.

Suppose you're a headhunter—someone who makes money by finding experienced people to move from one company to another. You're explaining to your new employees just what headhunters do. For a blueprint, you might say this: "I'll explain our three main tasks: finding job openings, finding employees, and matching employees with those openings."

Tip

Be sure to give your blueprint <u>after</u> you have defined your key term and given your bottom line. Otherwise, the blueprint will probably seem out of context to members of your audience—talking about how your talk is organized before they're fully sure what it's about.

Here's where the blueprint comes in your introduction:

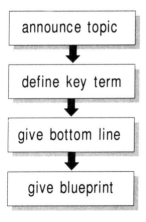

This technique—telling what you're about to cover—helps the audience stay on the same track you're on. Even though it's simple, it can go wrong. Here are some suggestions.

Give a blueprint for the body only

Don't confuse the outline of your presentation with a blueprint. A blueprint covers only the points in the *body* of the presentation.

All too often, I've seen speakers use something ineffective like this as the visual aid for their blueprint:

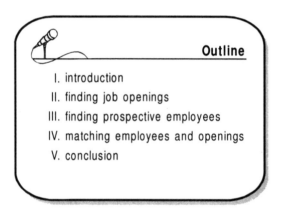

```
                                    Outline
    I. introduction
   II. finding job openings
  III. finding prospective employees
   IV. matching employees and openings
    V. conclusion
```

When the speaker turns to this visual aid, she finds herself saying something like this, "First, I'll give you an introduction. . . ." But she's already giving the introduction!

Then she'll continue, "And then I'll cover how to find job openings, how to find employees, how to match the two, and then I'll finish with some conclusions."

To avoid these problems, the visual aid would be better like this:

What Headhunters Do

- find job openings
- find prospective employees
- match employees and openings

So don't think of a blueprint as an outline of your entire presentation. The blueprint outlines only the body.

Tip

Be sure the order of the items in your blueprint is the same order as the sections of your presentation. And make sure your blueprint comes JUST before you start into your first section. Delays between a blueprint and the body of a presentation usually confuse the audience.

Avoid jargon in your blueprint

Jargon is the special vocabulary of a group of people. For people who share the jargon, there's no problem. But for those who don't, it can end communication.

Try to avoid inappropriate jargon in your blueprint. Too often, we see blueprints that really don't communicate much. Suppose the topic is learning about sailboats. This wouldn't be an effective blueprint for people who aren't especially familiar with sailing, would it?

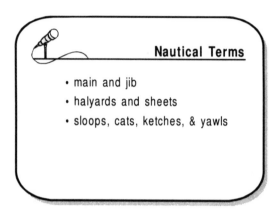

For people who aren't sailors, the blueprint doesn't say much more than "this presentation is going to talk about a lot of something or others."

This would probably be a better approach:

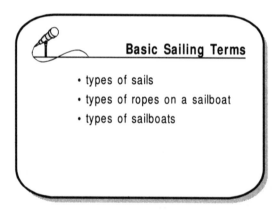

Don't always use a blueprint

A long or complicated blueprint can be more hindrance than help. For example, if your presentation has eight sections, a blueprint would seem awfully long. There's a good chance your audience could tune you out rather than listen to all eight items. Instead, simply use an implied blueprint: "I'll cover the eight retirement plans you can choose from." You haven't named the plans, but you have told your audience the structure you plan to follow.

Use strong transitions throughout

My third suggestion is to use strong transitions and plan them as you rehearse.

We know that good organization helps. So does a good blueprint. But all may be for nothing if listeners can't figure out when you've moved from one section of your presentation to the next.

Too often audiences perceive only this as the structure of the presentation they're attending:

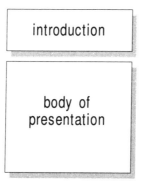

introduction

body of
presentation

That is, audiences usually know when they're in the introduction of a presentation and when they're in the body of it, but they seldom know where in the body of a presentation they are.

It would be better, then, if a speaker could communicate clearly the structure *within* the body of the presentation, like this:

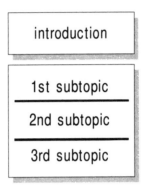

The key transition points are the places where a speaker moves from one subtopic to another—in other words, the bold horizontal lines in the illustration you just looked at.

In business writing, headings signal a new topic is coming up. In speaking, you must use other techniques. These are the three techniques I suggest:

- announce the transition explicitly

- use visual aids

- use body movement.

Announce the transition explicitly

Don't be afraid to be absolutely mechanical with your transitions. Subtlety may be nice in James Joyce's novels, but it's of little value in business presentations.

For an example, let's return to our topic on headhunters. This could be your first major transition:

- The first task for a headhunter is to find job openings to fill.

Then say what you have to say. When you're ready for the next item in your blueprint, say something like this:

- Now that we've found a job opening, we need to find someone to fill it. That brings me to our second task as headhunters.

Unmistakable. That's the "looking backward/looking forward" transition: it looks back at the section you just finished (finding jobs) and looks forward to the section you're about to start (finding employees).

This technique has a terrific advantage: it lets your audience know you're moving from one major point to another. Simply saying "next we'll look at . . ." would have been ambiguous: Were you moving from one *major* point to the next? Or were you moving from one *sub*point to the next?

With the "looking backward/looking forward" technique, your transition is clear. Your listeners know unmistakably that they've left one "town" and gone to the next.

Use visual aids to reinforce transitions

Explicitly announcing the transition is a good start, but you can reinforce your transition even more by using visual aids.

Suppose you use a visual aid near the beginning of your presentation to give your blueprint. You can use it again to move to each major point. That way, not only will your audience hear that you're making a transition—they can see it, too. You might even use highlighting on the visual aid to show the audience which point you're moving to:

Now it's easy for everyone to see what your next point is.

Use body movement to reinforce transitions

Finally, you can use your entire body to help reinforce a transition. If you're using a visual aid, move toward it and point to the next subtopic you're going to cover. If you're not using a visual aid, simply take a few steps to the side as you're announcing the next subtopic. Watch professional speakers. They often walk or make some other movement at key transition points.

To some, an obvious organization may seem terribly mechanical, but I think of it as wonderfully clear. And a clear organization doesn't squeeze the personality out of a presentation.

I've heard a fireman describe his first unsuccessful rescue—with a clear organization and tears in his listeners' eyes. I've heard a scientist describe a complex innovation for supercomputers—with a clear organization and the total attention of fellow scientists and laypeople alike. And I've heard a top general in the military update his senior officers—with a clear organization and the respectful, almost affectionate, response of his people.

So don't think of a clear organization as too mechanical. Think of it as a terrific way to communicate.

CHAPTER 19

Using examples

Bottom line

Use examples often—audiences will usually remember the points you make with examples longer than anything else.

The last chapter gave you a good structure for a presentation—now let's talk about content. I can't help you much with your particular topic, but I can point out where the content of presentations usually goes wrong: it's too abstract.

Far too often, presentations fail because the speaker uses generalizations but no examples. Chapter 7 talked about using examples in writing; this chapter will talk about examples for presentations.

Generalizations alone rarely communicate. In fact, there's some interesting research on this point. Researchers had people read abstract writing and try to figure it out. While they were reading, the people expressed their thoughts aloud ("Hmmm. Wonder what that means . . ."). That way, the researchers could observe the thinking process.

Guess what happened? When the people came across an abstract idea, they tried to think of an example. In other words, they tried to make the meaning clear by turning abstract statements they didn't understand into concrete ones they did.

As speakers, we're better off providing those examples ourselves. Examples take time, but not necessarily a lot. And there's no substitute for them when it comes to communication.

A close friend and respected communication consultant once said to me, "The two most common transitions in the language are *however* and *therefore*, but the most important is *for example.*"

Tip

> *As you design your presentation, check yourself: how often are you saying "for example" and "for instance"? And listen to other speakers, too. You'll notice the ones who use examples and the ones who don't.*

This chapter is composed almost entirely of examples, all from presentations I've seen. The examples were effective for me—I still remember them!

First we'll look at quick examples and then turn to longer ones.

Quick examples

Examples don't have to take more than a few seconds. Here are several quick ones:

- Applications are simply software programs—*like word processors, spreadsheets, or even computer bridge games.*

- Our department could save money if we stopped buying individual software packages and bought network versions instead. *For example, word processing software cost us about $5000 last year. But the network version of the same software would have cost us only $1200.*

- Our workshops are always small: *The class for new managers, for instance, is limited to 12 people. The class on new accounting methods is limited to 15.*

- We need to change some of the procedures in our store to improve its appearance. *For example, we inventory new merchandise at the sales counter—a messy procedure within view of the customer.*

Most of the communication actually takes place in the examples, doesn't it?

Tip

Generally put your key examples toward the front of your presentation. That's when the audience needs them. Too often, though, inexperienced speakers save the examples for the end.

Longer examples

Sometimes a short example just won't do. Either your topic is complex or you want the extra emphasis a longer example gives.

Here are three longer examples that speakers handled quite well. As you read them, try to imagine how little communication would have taken place with no examples at all—with only the abstract explanation.

Longer example 1: concurrent engineering

This example is from an engineer giving a presentation at a conference. Here is the abstract explanation of *concurrent engineering:* "designing an item, planning for its production, and planning for its maintenance all at the same time."

Fortunately, the speaker continued with an example:

> If you want a new part for a machine, the old way was to design the part, down to the last detail. Then the designers would give their design to the production people who would prepare tools to make it. Once the part was actually in production, the maintenance people would begin doing repairs or preventive maintenance. That was inefficient.
>
> Concurrent engineering plans for *all three stages* at the same time. The production people work with the designers, perhaps pointing out that their tools would have great difficulty rounding out an edge to the designers' specifications. But a slightly different edge would be easy.
>
> The maintenance people might point out that a component that fails every 75 hours is in a place that requires removing 15 bolts to get to it. Redesigning would make their job easier.
>
> Having the designers, the producers, and the maintainers work together—concurrently—makes engineering far more efficient. And the product can be much less expensive for its life cycle—perhaps slightly more expensive to design, but cheaper to produce and cheaper to maintain.

The example is effective, isn't it? It would take a minute to present, but I can't think of a shorter way to communicate the concept.

Longer example 2: live-fire vulnerability testing

The next example is from a research analyst. Here's an abstract explanation of *live-fire vulnerability testing:* "finding out what happens to our military weapon systems when enemy weapons hit them."

When I first heard this term, I was mentally searching for a concrete example. Fortunately, the speaker supplied it:

Suppose there's a new tank, and we want to find out what might happen if an enemy missile hits it. People in the military don't want to wait for an actual war to get the answer.

So they get a new tank and actually shoot at it. The tank is fully equipped for battle—loaded with fuel and its own weapons (of course, there aren't any people in it). The missiles they shoot at the tank are similar to the kind the enemy would actually shoot.

The cost is an expensive tank, but the information from the test is often invaluable. Researchers can find out how vulnerable the tank is to the enemy's weapons and possibly make changes to improve it.

The soldiers who operate tanks certainly favor this type of testing.

There you have it: the example. The audience is now ready to hear more about live-fire vulnerability testing. Without the example, they might have preferred being in that tank.

Longer example 3: adapting physical education for children with special needs

This example is from a curriculum coordinator. Here is the abstract explanation of *adapting physical education for children with special needs:* "creating games during physical education for children who are unable to participate in the regular games children play."

Unlike the earlier terms, we can understand that definition fairly easily, but it has little impact. However, the speaker wanted more than intellectual understanding. She wanted us to *feel* the need for her program.

So she was creative—she involved us in a living example. First, she asked for a volunteer to come to the front of the room. Then she asked him to run to the other end of the room, pick up a bean bag, and return. That's typical of a game elementary school students might play.

Next, she asked the volunteer to put on a blindfold. She then asked members of the audience to suggest ways to adapt the game for him. One person suggested holding his arm while he walked. Another suggested handing the bean bags to the "blind person" when he reached the other end of the room. That way, the blindfolded volunteer wouldn't have trouble finding them.

Then the game took place again, the runner blindfolded, the other volunteers participating. It was fun to watch, fun for the blindfolded volunteer, fun for the other volunteers. I suspect it would have been fun for elementary school students participating with a person who was actually blind.

This was a terrific example. By seeing the blindfolded person, we were all able to empathize. We understood what "adapting physical education for children with special needs" meant, and we understood its value, too.

This was also a good way to involve the audience. We'll look further at this in Chapter 25, "Involving your audience and using humor."

Examples may seem simple to the speaker, but they're often crucial for the audience. So consciously look for places for examples: quick ones take almost no time and can be extremely important; longer ones not only help communication but provide extra emphasis, too.

CHAPTER 20

Remembering what to say

Bottom line

Well-designed visual aids greatly reduce the pressure of remembering what to say in your presentation.

A speaker's greatest fear: going blank with everybody staring. You try to think of something—anything!—but your brain seems to be disconnected.

What can you do?

Nothing. At that point, it's too late. But you can do something to avoid being in that situation (other than declining invitations to speak). You can design a way of remembering the content of your presentation so going blank almost never happens. And if it does—which is unlikely—you'll have something to help you get going again.

That's what this chapter is about. My recommendation is that you try to use visual aids for almost all speaking situations. If they're well designed, they'll help not only your audience—they'll help you, too.

But to see the value of visual aids, let's consider all four common ways of remembering material:

- memorizing

- reading from a complete text

- using notes
- using visual aids as notes

Memorizing

Memorizing is absolutely the worst way to keep track of your material.

People who memorize almost always are preoccupied with the *words* they're saying—not with the *ideas* behind those words (or with the audience). As a result, normal inflection disappears. And, worse, those terrible blank moments become almost inevitable.

I used to memorize the first few sentences of my introduction, just so I'd get off to a good start. But I found that I almost always fumbled those lines. Now when I speak, I'm very familiar with what I want to say, but I'm familiar with the *ideas* rather than with the exact words. When I rehearse, I use similar words to express my ideas, but I don't use exactly the same words each time.

Even top professional actors can have trouble with memorized speeches. Just watch the Academy Awards. I suggest you avoid memorizing.

Reading from a complete text

Ask audiences what they most hate about presentations, and someone is sure to say, "Having people stand up and just read to me. If that's all they were going to do, I could have read it myself."

Why is reading a presentation hard to do well?

Most of us have suffered through people reading badly. Here are some reasons that happens:

- *The speaker loses normal inflection.* Like people who have memorized their speech, people who read aloud often lose touch with the ideas behind the words. You can easily tell if that happens: listen for pauses. Natural speaking is filled with them; unnatural reading isn't.

- *The text isn't spoken language.* Too often speakers write their speeches in "businessese"—that difficult gobbledygook that's hard enough for us to read, much less listen to.

- *The speaker is static.* The potted plant will probably move more. There is little movement, little energy, little visual interest behind the lectern.

- *There's no eye contact.* Any eye contact is with the text, not with the audience. Gestures are limited to adjusting eyeglasses.

- *The speaker is scared.* Often speakers decide to read their speech because they're afraid to try anything else. They know that reading will fail, but at least it will fail with a small "f" rather than a capital one.

But reading isn't always bad. (Just almost always.) Sometimes speakers simply have to read: they're announcing a precise policy; timing a short presentation down to the second; talking to speakers of English as a second language and avoiding colloquialisms; or attempting the kind of eloquence that rarely happens without the exact words. Fortunately, there are some ways for reading aloud to be successful.

Some suggestions for reading aloud

Good readers can overcome the problems I just mentioned. Here's what I suggest if you must read your presentation:

- *Inflection.* To make your words sound natural, rehearse often. Check yourself for pauses. Ask yourself if your words sound the way you'd say them. This is surprisingly hard to do—you'll probably have to work at it.

- *Spoken language.* You can also improve your inflection by choosing words you might actually say—rather than using "businessese." In fact, top speech writers work to put colloquialisms in the text: "Okay, let's push that idea a little farther and see what we come up with" or "I think this new approach will be easier once we get the hang of it."

- *Movement.* Plan for key gestures: pointing in the general direction of the city you're mentioning, showing how big or how small something is, shrugging at the right time, raising an eyebrow. Some speakers put cues for these gestures in their text.

- *Eye contact.* If your text is "user friendly," you have a better chance of looking at your audience. So you need a good layout for your text. You don't want bunches of long paragraphs, or you'll lose your place every time you look up. Instead, try starting a new paragraph after every sentence or two. And avoid all capital letters, which are hard to read. Instead, use upper and lower case in a larger type size.

Tip

The audience can get distracted by watching speakers turn the pages of their text. Instead, use unstapled pages and simply slide the page you've finished to the side.

A good example

Picture a graduation speech: dull, boring, the audience half asleep. It doesn't have to be that way. I once saw a graduation speaker do a terrific job, and he read the entire address aloud, holding the audience spellbound.

How did he succeed?

- First, his text was extraordinarily witty and in spoken English.

- Second, he was energetic—gesturing constantly, varying the loudness of his voice, even singing the French national anthem in English (to illustrate a point).

- Third, his eyes were piercing. We had the feeling he was looking at us constantly. Finally, he wasn't a bit scared of us. The auditorium was his, and he ruled it totally.

But don't read your presentation

As far as I'm concerned, reading well requires me to work too hard at the wrong time: when I'm actually giving my presentation. I have to be constantly aware of my gestures, inflection, eye contact—things that come naturally when I'm just talking. That's why bad speech readers are common and good ones are rare. Talking normally is usually much more effective.

Tip

If you expect to be nervous, try reading the first words of your presentation—especially a funny or moving quotation. That way, you'll take lots of pressure off the most nervous time of all: the beginning. But then move quickly away from reading—preferably to visual aids. In fact, the quotation can be your first visual aid.

Let's turn now to what used to be the most common technique for remembering material.

Using notes

Using notes is normally better than reading: speakers can have normal inflection and make eye contact more easily. However, if the notes are on a lectern, speakers probably won't move very far from it. And if the notes are in their hands, they won't gesture much. Also, there's that constant looking down at the notes. That doesn't happen when speakers use visual aids correctly—when the speaker looks at the visual aid, the audience should be looking there, too.

Some suggestions for using notes

If you must use notes, here are some suggestions:

- *Use note cards.* They're small and easy to handle.

- *Don't put much on them.* What would you use as headings or sub-headings if you had written your entire presentation? That's what should go on your note cards—not lots of text. Too many notes get in the way of good eye contact.

- *Leave your notes on the lectern or table and move away from them occasionally.* During parts of your presentation when you're especially confident, move around to gain rapport with your audience. You can rehearse when to do this.

Tip

Be sure to put these items on your note cards: quotations, statistics, and lists. We've all seen speakers have trouble thinking of that last item in the list they're giving.

A good example

I once saw a woman who was excellent at speaking from notes. She'd start by glancing at them, then leave them on the lectern and walk to the center of the stage where she'd simply talk. When she finished her point, she'd walk quietly back to the lectern, glance at her notes, and return to the center of the stage.

You might think she looked strange walking quietly back to the lectern. On the contrary, we were much more aware of her walking back toward us. The feeling was that she, like most human beings, needed some reminders of what to say. But she wasn't going to let that interfere with talking to us.

Using visual aids as notes

Now for the technique I've been referring to all along: visual aids. Today they are by far the most common way to remember what to say. Let's consider an example.

I once saw a person explain his tasks as a desk editor for a major news magazine. He spoke for about ten minutes using four visual aids. This was his first one (his blueprint):

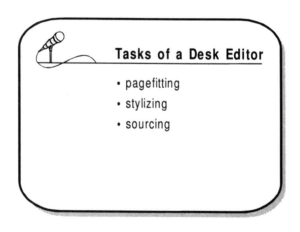

He briefly defined *desk editor* and the three terms on his visual aid. He didn't need to remember what to say during his introduction—because the first visual aid served as his notes!

Then he turned to his next visual aid:

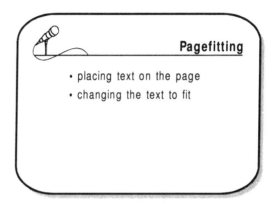

During this part, he gave us examples for each point.

When he had said all he had to, he didn't need to worry what was next. He simply turned to his next visual aid:

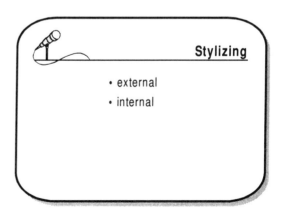

Again, this was all he needed to remember what to say. The examples he'd rehearsed came right to mind.

By now, you can imagine what his final visual aid looked like:

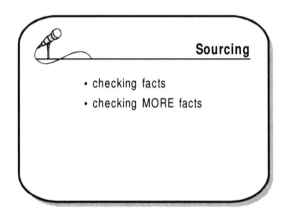

These may seem so simple and obvious, but that's the point: the simple visual aids served as the headings and sub-headings he might have used if he'd written down his entire presentation.

When he spoke, he'd come to a "heading," say what he wanted to, and move on. If he forgot something he'd intended to say, that was all right. The audience would never know.

This technique of using visual aids as notes has these important advantages:

- *You don't have to worry about what you're going to say next.* This is a *significant* advantage. Your next visual aid has your next major idea. Just turn to it when you're ready. That way, your mind isn't constantly cluttered by the fear that you may forget what's next.

- *You can move about the room.* Inexperienced speakers don't want to move, but movement helps you relax and adds energy to your presentation. We'll talk more about this in Chapter 28, "Using effective techniques of delivery."

- *You can have good eye contact with your audience.* You can look at your audience all the time—except when you're looking briefly at your visual aid. But that's okay; the audience will look at your visual aid then, too.

- *Your audience feels comfortable knowing you're on your planned track.* Well-designed visual aids show that you have a plan and are following it.

Tip

Your visual aids don't need to be only word charts: diagrams, pictures, and graphs all give structure to a section of your presentation and serve well as notes for you. Chapter 23, "Designing visual aids—further tips," can give you some ideas.

✢   ✢   ✢

Five other chapters discuss visual aids:

- Chapter 21, "Choosing visual aids," talks about the different kinds available—from overhead transparencies to flip charts—and the advantages and disadvantages of each.

- Chapter 22, "Designing visual aids," then suggests ways to prepare your visuals so they'll look good and be effective.

- Chapter 23, "Designing visual aids—further tips," continues Chapter 22.

- Chapter 24, "Designing computer presentations," suggests some special considerations for using the extra power of computers.

- Chapter 29, "Presenting visual aids," gives some do's and don't's for handling visual aids during your presentation.

CHAPTER 21

Choosing visual aids

Bottom line

Don't always use the same type of visual aid—each type has its own strengths and weaknesses.

Some older books on speechmaking cautioned against visual aids: "Don't rely on them too much," they'd say. "Don't use them as crutches." But the standard for those books was the immobile speaker standing behind a lectern, declaiming to the audience for 30 minutes.

Things have changed.

Today, almost all business speakers use visual aids. One reason is technology: many of us can produce them rather easily at work. Another is that we've learned their advantages—for us (as speakers) and for our audiences:

- They keep *us* aware of where we are in our presentation.

- They keep *the audience* aware of where we are in our presentation.

- They visually reinforce our words: the audience can see an idea and hear about it at the same time.

- They emphasize important ideas.

Once you get used to speaking with visual aids, you'll rarely want to speak without them. The advantages are too important.

This chapter will help you choose the best type of visual aid for your presentation. We'll consider the advantages and disadvantages of these (the most common types people use):

- overhead transparencies
- 35-millimeter slides
- computer presentations
- flip charts
- blackboards and whiteboards
- objects and models
- imaginary visual aids
- handouts as visual aids

By the way, if you find that speaking is a significant part of your job, you'll certainly want to investigate computer presentations.

They used to be the future, but now they're the present.

Overhead transparencies

This is certainly the most common type of visual aid for business presentations—and, not surprisingly, the favorite of many speakers.

It requires only an overhead projector, a screen (or even a wall), and transparencies. Virtually all conference rooms are equipped for them.

Advantages of overhead transparencies

- *Transparencies are easy to make.* Simply prepare your visual aid on paper and then copy it on a copier. But instead of copying onto blank paper, copy onto a transparency. This way you can make transparencies quickly, revise them quickly, and revise them often. You can also make them yourself, without waiting for a professional staff to produce them for you. This convenience often translates into whether people update their presentations or let them go stale.

- *They're cheap.* They cost only pennies a copy.

- *They're portable.* For most presentations, you can easily fit your transparencies in your briefcase with room to spare. This is no small matter if you travel often. If you use cardboard frames around your transparencies, you increase the bulk somewhat, but they're still quite portable.

- *They let you be flexible.* You can rearrange your presentation on the fly—with the audience staring at you— to meet new needs. For example, occasionally someone needs an answer now for something you planned to cover later. No problem: just reach for the appropriate transparency and press ahead.

- *You can write on them.* Sometimes you don't want the audience to see a static visual aid (like a ready-made equation); instead, you want to create it, step by step, as the audience watches. With a transparency, you can do that easily. Some pens are designed for that purpose. An added advantage is that you can easily erase your writing later with a damp paper towel (if you're like me, however, you may walk around for a day or so with red or green or blue fingers).

- *You can see what's next.* Since most speakers handle their own transparencies, they can glance at the label on the next one and see what the next topic is. That's a really important advantage; otherwise, part of your mind is constantly trying to remember what's next. Sneak glances are no problem with overheads.

- *They can look extremely professional.* Color printers and copiers can enhance your message by drawing attention to key features and providing a visually interesting (yet still unobtrusive) background. You can also reproduce colorful photographs on a transparency and have good resolution.

- *They can be informal if necessary.* For an impromptu meeting with colleagues, you can simply hand print or hand draw your transparencies.

Disadvantages of using overhead transparencies

Alas, the world isn't perfect. Here are some of the disadvantages of using overhead transparencies:

- *The projector may not be very good.* Because overhead transparencies are the most popular visual aid, the equipment takes a beating. You'll often find projectors that don't focus well, have dim bulbs, or have no bulbs at all. That's why I carry my own projector for local presentations. When I travel, I insist in advance on a good projector. Then, when I arrive at the place for my presentation, I go immediately to the projector and try it out. If it's not good, I try to get another one.

- *The bulb can burn out.* Many of today's projectors have a spare bulb built in, but sometimes the spare is burned out, too. Presenters who have a bulb burn out switch to the spare and go on. They usually forget to tell the visual aids people that the overhead is now down to only one good bulb. If that one burns out, you're left with none.

Many speakers consider the overhead transparency their first choice of visual aid unless they have a good reason not to use it. But there are many good reasons to use other visual aids, either separately or in conjunction with overhead transparencies.

35-millimeter slides

Advantages of 35-millimeter slides

Thirty-five-millimeter slides can produce wonderfully professional presentations. You can show colorful word charts and colorful pictures, too. Audiences love real pictures— of things, people, even themselves. NASA has a speaker's bureau that uses slides, and you can imagine the beautiful photographs of space walks, the Earth, and rockets taking off.

If you want a thoroughly professional look with high resolution, slides are the way to go. They're also especially useful for standard presentations that many people give. For example, a woman I knew owned a business selling light fixtures. She made 35-millimeter slides of the fixtures her company had actually installed, and then she built her standard sales presentation around those slides. All her marketing reps used copies of that standard presentation.

Once slides are in the tray (right side up, facing the right direction) they stay right—and in the proper sequence. There is little fuss to handling them other than clicking a button to change to the next one.

Disadvantages of 35-millimeter slides

However, there are some disadvantages to using 35-millimeter slides. The most significant is that making them normally requires professional help. That means they're usually expensive and hard to revise.

They also usually take longer to make. And they're also virtually impossible to rearrange during a presentation.

Also important, the lights normally should be dimmer in the room for a slide show than for transparencies. That's restful for your audience. *Very* restful. And sometimes the lights in a room can be only all the way on or all the way off. With 35-millimeter slides, you'll have to turn the lights all the way off. As a result, the audience can't see you, and you can't see the audience. The effect is not good.

Finally, 35-millimeter slide projectors aren't nearly as common in conference rooms as overhead projectors, so you may have to carry your own. And if there is one there, it may have problems with jamming, focus, or burned out bulbs—and no spare projector.

Tip

> *Use 35-millimeter slides sparingly. They normally look great only when the lights are too dim for the audience and for you. This is a <u>significant</u> problem, possible, but hard, to overcome.*

Computer presentations

Computer presentations are becoming ever more popular. Essentially, they project either onto a large monitor or through an overhead projector onto a screen. Many organizations have the equipment—even special rooms—for these presentations.

Advantages of computer presentations

If you're showing what a computer program can do, computer presentations are indispensable. And they're also useful replacements for overhead projectors, 35-millimeter slides, and even flip charts. They show color well, are very easy to create and modify, and can look highly professional. They are superb for animating your visual aids—for example, adding bullets step by step to a chart.

They can also be wonderful for doing "what if" presentations—perhaps using a graph, changing some values, and having a formula calculate a new result. For example, in a presentation on sales projections, you could change the projected sales figures in front of your audience's eyes, and everyone could then see the effect on your company's bottom line.

You can easily add graphics called "clip art"—pre-drawn figures you simply cut and paste into your computer presentation. Chapter 23, "Designing visual aids—further tips," has an example of clip art.

Computer presentations are very handy for standard (perhaps daily or weekly) presentations when data changes but format doesn't. The effort to prepare the computer presentation the first time is repaid ever after because updating the data—and, hence, the presentation—becomes simple.

Automated computer presentations are also handy at conventions when roving audiences stop in randomly. The computer show draws the crowd and keeps going longer than most human beings can. Also, for such shows, you can design participation: the user answers a question or pushes a button for some action.

Finally, you can have a wealth of backup material in your computer and call on it instantly if the need arises.

Tip

Use a computer presentation if you want that "profes-sional look." Or to show how a computer works or to put on a continuous display for an audience.

Disadvantages of computer presentations

Computer presentations depend on technology, so there's more to go wrong. And if something goes wrong with the equipment, you'll be pretty well stuck. Also, if you don't have good equipment, the projected image can be fuzzy or visible only to a narrow segment of the room. Even with good equipment, the room may be fairly dark.

The equipment—a computer (possibly portable) and a projection unit—is expensive, fragile, and awkward to carry (if it isn't set up permanently where you'll give your pre-sentation). The equipment can also be time-consuming to set up and adjust.

The biggest disadvantage of computer presentations is the potential for real-time glitches not possible in other me-dia. If you press the wrong key or enter the wrong data, the result may be unrecoverable. Back-up transparencies are often a good idea.

Nevertheless, computer presentations can be terrific. I be-lieve the advantages often clearly outweigh the disadvan-tages. The key is to use the full power of your computer. Chapter 24 gives suggestions on how to design computer presentations.

Flip charts

Flip charts are very large tablets of paper on an easel.

Advantages of flip charts

Flip charts are useful for creating a visual aid "before your audience's very eyes." That is, you can start with a blank page, ask for the audience's ideas, and record those ideas on the flip chart. The effect is that you have your "sleeves rolled up" and are ready to get to work.

You can begin a presentation by making a list of what people in the audience want to talk about—they enjoy having you discuss and then check off their ideas. You can even have a volunteer come to the front of the room and record the audience's ideas.

Flip charts are also cheap, easy to make (even in advance), and easy to revise. You can tear off the pages and tape them around the room for later reference. Some people, particularly in informal presentations, put their blueprint on a flip chart and leave it in view. Then they use overhead transparencies or some other means for the main part of their presentation. When they're ready to move to another section of their presentation, they simply walk over to the flip chart, point out the next item on the blueprint, and move on.

Flip charts are also easy ways to use color—simply have a handful of colorful pens and you can put your artistry to work. Some speakers like to make all headings one color and all text or bullets another.

Tip

Use a flip chart for a "sleeves up" approach when you have a small audience and want to record the audience's ideas during your presentation. Or use it if you want to keep the pages on display around the room.

Disadvantages of flip charts

The main disadvantage is that flip charts won't work for large audiences—those sitting in the back of the room may not be able to see them. If your audience is small, you have no problem. They're also cumbersome to carry around, and they're hard to save or reuse. The pages sometimes crinkle—noisily—when you fold them back. And they require an easel (not always available), which makes a nice object for people to back into or trip over.

Flip charts also usually look homemade and depend on relatively neat handwriting (legible, at least).

If you're writing on a flip chart during your presentation, you may have trouble writing neatly and talking at the same time. And even if you're a good speller, your hurry to put words on the page in front of your audience may cause a handwritten "typo." (Or "thinko," as I've heard them called.) Then that misspelled word will stay in front of your audience's eyes, constantly distracting them. Also, the writing from colored pens can bleed through to several sheets beneath.

Tip

When using a flip chart, leave one or two blank pages after every page you write on. That will avoid showing the bleed-through that occurs. You may also want to put tabs on the pages you plan to use. That way you won't have to turn a number of blank pages to get to the one you want.

Blackboards and whiteboards

Blackboards and whiteboards have essentially the same advantages and disadvantages as flip charts (except you can't pack a blackboard and take it with you, and you can't page back and forth). I especially like whiteboards because they lighten the room and show color well.

The biggest caution for whiteboards is the pen: some pens are intended for whiteboards and erase easily; some don't erase—ever—and give memorable indigestion to visual aids people. In fact, visual aids people try not to allow permanent marking pens in the same room with a whiteboard.

If you're using a whiteboard, check the pens in advance. Otherwise, you may be embarrassed when you try to erase the board and find—behold!—the words just stay there, giving a whole new meaning to "my words will live forever." You'll want to slink quietly off.

Objects and models

Sometimes there's simply no replacement for an object itself. If it's small (like a new kind of light bulb), there's no reason to have pictures or diagrams of it. Just show the light bulb.

If it's large, like a new building—or tiny, like an atom—a model can be the highlight of your presentation: professional looking and interesting.

Tip

Don't pass an object around the audience. You'll be creating your own greatest distraction: people looking at the object simply won't be paying attention to you. Just hold the object up or walk quickly around the room with it. If it's not fragile or expensive, consider leaving it on display for a few minutes after your presentation.

Imaginary visual aids

Yes, some of the most creative visual aids I've seen in presentations haven't even existed. Here are some examples of imaginary visual aids:

- One person was showing the distance someone could broad jump. So she made the stage an imaginary place for the event, started at one edge, and walked the distance for the high school record. She talked about that awhile, then moved a little farther to show the collegiate record. And so on.

- Another person turned the stage into a boat. He showed us where starboard was, the stern, and so on. He used the stage as his reference throughout his presentation.

- Another made the stage an airport, showing which directions the planes would take off and land, where the gates were, and where the control tower was. She then used this to illustrate the various traffic patterns the planes would fly, depending on the direction the wind was blowing.

Such creativity isn't too informal: these speakers were in relatively formal situations, and their creativity added liveliness and interest.

Handouts as visual aids

An all too common visual aid is the handout. Inexperienced speakers often pass one out even when there's no immediate need. The result is a major distraction. Simply look around the room, and you'll often see people leafing through the handout rather than looking at the speaker.

In fact, Jim Casimir, a top executive, says, "A good rule is *never* use a handout during your presentation."

If you *must* use a handout during your presentation, I suggest these steps:

- Pass out the handout yourself, counting out the right number for each row. That's faster than dropping off a bunch at one side of the room and waiting for copies to get to everyone. In a large room or auditorium, ask several members of the audience to help you. You can increase their efficiency by giving them specific instructions: "Please take the left side and count out the correct number for each row. Thanks."

- Go through the handout as a group, pointing out what, specifically, the audience needs to look at. That way, everyone's attention will be focused.

- When you're through, ask members to set the handout aside. I say something like this: "Okay, we're through with the handout, so if you'll set it aside, we'll move on." Audiences rarely seem to feel dictated to. They simply set the handout aside and look up.

Some organizations are used to passing out a paper copy of their visual aids to the audience. If possible, do that at the end of the presentation. That way the audience isn't distracted.

We've covered many kinds of visual aids, each with advantages and disadvantages. The next two chapters offer suggestions on how to design them.

CHAPTER 22

Designing visual aids

Bottom line

Simply having visual aids is a good start, but having <u>well-designed</u> visual aids can make all the difference.

This chapter deals with the fine points of designing visual aids that look good and help you and your audience. I'll concentrate on the overhead transparency, because it's the most common visual aid and because the fundamentals for it apply to other visual aids, too.

And, as you'll see when you get to Chapter 24, the fundamentals here apply fully to designing computer presentations, too.

Some organizations have standard formats for their visual aids. But lots of organizations don't. In fact, you may be your own typist, graphic artist, typographer, and photocopier. Many of us are. If so, this chapter will help you design your own visual aids well. If others do your typing and designing, this will help you tell them what you want.

Margaret Raab, in *The Presentation Design Book,* says that "good graphic design is invisible." So true. For most occasions, we don't want the audience to gasp with pleasure at eye-catching visual aids. Instead, we want them to concentrate on the content—to pay attention to *what* we're saying rather than to *how* we're saying it.

Keith Thompson, in *PC Publishing and Presentations*, expresses a similar idea: "Your slides should reinforce your message, not overshadow it. To put it another way: the speaker needs to remain the center of interest, not the slides."

Of course, there are exceptions. It's fine to show off a little. But you'll usually want your visual aids to have straightforward efficiency.

Here are suggestions for designing efficient visual aids:

- Use a title transparency.
- Put the words near the top of each transparency.
- Don't use too many words for each idea.
- Don't put several ideas on the same transparency.
- Use upper and lower case.
- Use large letters.
- Use a sans serif font.
- Use a single orientation: all landscape or all portrait.
- Add some color.
- Usually avoid borders.
- Place logos effectively.
- Consider using frames to hold your transparencies.
- Label your transparencies.

Let's look at each of these more closely.

Use a title transparency

Your first transparency should have at least the title of your presentation and your name on it.

Tip

If the title of your presentation has unfamiliar terms in it, you may want to leave the title transparency on while you define those terms. I've seen people spend two or three useful minutes on the title transparency before moving to the next one.

Some speakers decide to replace their name on their title transparency with the name of the person or organization they're speaking to.

That's normally not a good idea: members of the audience know who *they* are, but they don't necessarily know who *you* are. They'll be happy to see your name so they'll know how to refer to you during the presentation.

By the way, I suggest you use the name you want people to call you: "Ed Bailey" instead of "Edward Bailey" or "Professor Joan Hiller" instead of "Professor J. Hiller."

Tip

You might want to have a test transparency—all mine says is "test transparency   test transparency   test transparency. . . ." That way, when you're testing the overhead projector and some members of the audience are in the room, they won't see one of your actual transparencies.

Be sure to use typical type sizes on your test transparency, including your smallest type size.

Put the words near the top

Most of us like the symmetrical appearance when we center things, so naturally we want to center the words (or diagrams, or pictures) on our transparencies or other visual aids.

Centering often looks nice on an unprojected transparency and on the paper copy we use to run a transparency. But keep in mind that audiences can't always see all the screen—those in the back may be able to see only the top of it.

So I always work from the top of my transparency, because the top of the screen is visible to everybody in the room. That is, I center my text from left to right but not from top to bottom.

In other words, not like this:

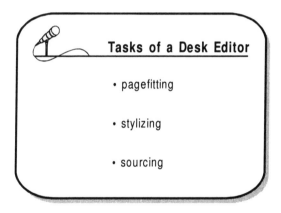

Tasks of a Desk Editor

• pagefitting

• stylizing

• sourcing

I think of the top of the screen as "golden" space I want to make the best use of. (Experience has been my teacher on this!)

So here's the way I would actually design that transparency:

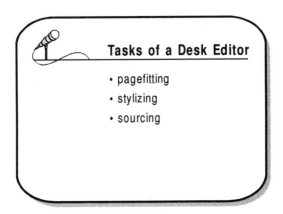

Putting the words on the top doesn't make the transparency appear distorted or off-balance, does it?

You may think you can just push the transparency up on the projector during your presentation. But that's one more thing to think about and can seem awkward. Instead, just keep your words and images high.

Don't use too many words for each idea

Perhaps the most common mistake is putting too much material on visual aids.

The temptation is to put everything there: that way, you won't forget anything.

But if you put everything you have to say on your transparency, you'll end up reading it aloud, turning to your next one, reading that, and so forth—leaving nothing else for you to say. Audiences don't appreciate hearing speakers read most of their presentation.

Here is a transparency with wall-to-wall words:

What Headhunters Do

- The first task headhunters do is find openings in other companies. These openings should normally be for relatively senior people who have special skills or academic qualifications.
- The second task is to find prospective employees to fill those job openings. In addition to good paper qualifications, they must be effective managers; otherwise, companies won't use our headhunters.
- Finally, headhunters must match employees and openings to make sure there's a good fit.

Instead, choose a few key words to serve as reminders. As I mentioned earlier, these reminders are like the headings and sub-headings you might use if you'd written your entire presentation.

Here's a revision, this time with only brief verb phrases as reminders:

What Headhunters Do

- find job openings
- find prospective employees
- match employees and openings

You've now left something to say, so you won't just be reading aloud. This isn't a small point.

Most presentations by inexperienced speakers have far too many words on the transparencies. That virtually guarantees problems: the audience won't want to read the transparencies because they look cluttered. And if the speaker does nothing but read transparencies, the audience gets upset.

That's not to say that transparencies must have only simple phrases on them. Short sentences are okay, especially for questions and brief quotations.

Just work for less rather than more—let phrases be the norm and full sentences be the exception.

Tip

Some organizations encourage speakers to leave a paper copy of their visual aids with the audience. As a result, speakers tend to make the visual aids self-explanatory so the paper copies will stand alone. The actual visual aids then become much too wordy. Instead, make your visual aids the best you can for your presentation, then annotate the paper copies to help them stand alone.

Don't put several ideas on the same transparency

Another common mistake is putting too many ideas on the same transparency.

This happens often with beginning speakers. But, as with other things, less is often more. Here's a busy transparency from a presentation on expert systems:

Mechanical expert system
   Symptoms: the engine won't start, the lights are
   off, the radio won't play
   Solution: recharge or replace the battery

Medical expert system
   Symptoms: runny nose, sore throat, coughing
   Solution: the patient has a cold

See how cluttered that looks?

Just because material can fit on a transparency doesn't mean it should be there. A simple transparency focuses the audience's attention on those few simple points. A cluttered transparency, on the other hand, may distract so much that the audience doesn't focus anywhere at all.

So let's take each section of the cluttered transparency and put it on its own transparency. Here's what the same words on two transparencies could look like:

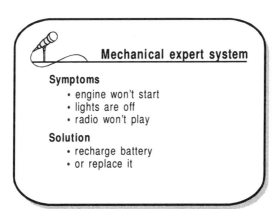

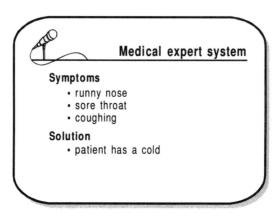

By using two transparencies, you can also improve the layout—adding white space and bullets.

Use upper and lower case

Before computers, which can easily vary type size, speakers often used all upper case (capital letters) on transparencies. That was the only way a typewriter could make words large enough. Today, however, researchers believe that a page entirely in upper case type is hard to read:

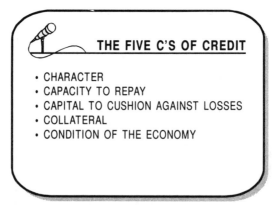

Instead of using all upper case to get larger letters, just use mainly lower case in a larger type size:

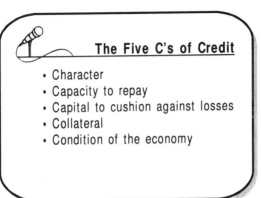

Use large letters

Looks can be deceiving. What looks plenty large on the transparency you're holding in your hand can look awfully small once you project it on the screen. Too often speakers wait until the actual presentation before testing their transparencies—then look with shock at the small letters.

Inevitably, they mutter something like, "I hope you all can read this." That doesn't make for a strong start, and it throws the speaker off guard, too.

There isn't any right type size to use because:

- projectors have different focal lengths

- the size of the projection on the screen depends on how far the projector is from it

- in a large room people may be farther from the screen than in a small room

Even though these variables exist, I rarely use a type size smaller than 20 points. I normally use 28 points or larger. In case you're not familiar with point sizes, here are samples:

This is 20-point type.

This is 28-point type.

Use a sans serif font

Terms like *points* and *serifs* were alien to most of us a few years ago, but the computer revolution for word processing has made the terms more common and given us the ability to put them into practice.

As I mentioned earlier in the book, serifs are those little lines that hang down from the crossbar of a *T*, stick out from the sides of an *H*, etc. But some typefaces (called *sans serif*) don't have those lines. Here are examples of both kinds:

Serif: **THEIR**   their

Sans serif: THEIR   their

The standard for visual aids is a sans serif typeface. This is the opposite of the standard for documents, which use a serif typeface for text (as in this book), reserving sans serif for some headings. For a transparency, though, sans serif projects a cleaner, less cluttered image on the screen. I use it almost exclusively in my visual aids.

Use a single orientation

There are two basic orientations for your slides: landscape and portrait. Think about the pictures you might see in an art gallery. Landscape means the transparency is wider than it is tall:

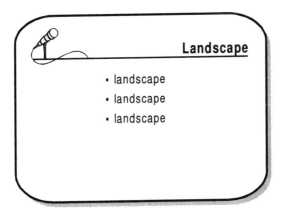

That's the orientation you'd expect for landscape paintings, too: wider than they are tall. On the other hand, picture those grim-faced, serious portraits you've seen of bewigged forefathers—taller than they are wide:

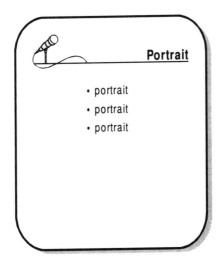

The standard for presentations is landscape, but either orientation is acceptable:

- Portrait has space at the bottom of the transparency that projects too low on the screen. That's fine. Just keep your content on the top two-thirds of the transparency.

- Landscape is so wide that a line of text going all the way across the transparency would be too long. Be sure to use generous margins.

Basically, landscape and portrait both give you the coverage on the screen you need. The problem is they give you *more* than you need. Landscape gives you too much width; portrait gives you too much length. But if you place your words well, either orientation will do.

Tip

Try not to have some transparencies in landscape and some in portrait. Your presentation will look inconsistent.

Add some color

Color can make your presentation look professional and, used carefully, help reinforce your message. Frankly, it's a must today except for informal presentations. Black-and-white presentations are going the way of black-and-white television.

Here are a couple of tips for using color:

- *Normally use a light background.* A light background lightens the room and lets you use other colors on the visual aid effectively. That is, your audience's eyes will go right to the colored image on the screen when the background is light.

- *Use colors for your logo and title section of every transparency.* This will guarantee a splash of color on every transparency. You'll find this color won't distract: it soon becomes a nearly invisible presence that simply brightens up every transparency.

- *Use colors consistently.* Don't just design terrific visual aids; instead, design a terrific *set* of visual aids. Give titles, headings, etc., consistent colors throughout.

Tip

If you don't want the expense of printing color transparencies, consider writing on an occasional transparency with the color markers designed for such a purpose.

Usually avoid borders

Borders are those nice looking lines that form edging around a page:

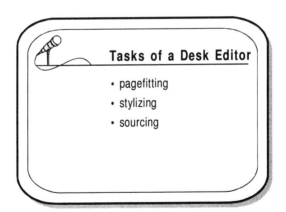

The problem is that what looks nice on paper and nice on a transparency in your hands looks bad when projected:

most conference rooms and screens aren't set up so everyone in the room can see the entire transparency.

So the audience doesn't see a nice border; the audience sees only *part* of a nice border. The rest is cut off. I suggest not adding a border to the transparency itself.

Place logos effectively

An earlier part of this chapter pointed out the value of the top part of a transparency—the part virtually everybody in the audience can see.

Yet many companies have, as part of their style guide, a requirement to have the company's logo or name take up the top 20% of the transparency. That doesn't leave enough room for the transparency's title and actual content.

Notice all the wasted space when the company's name is at the top:

EDITORIAL CONSULTANTS, INC.

Tasks of a Desk Editor

- pagefitting
- stylizing
- sourcing

I suggest putting the company's logo or name on the same line as the transparency's title. (For an example, look at most of the samples in this book.) That way, you'll have plenty of space for your content.

Consider using frames

Some speakers tape each transparency to a cardboard or plastic frame. That's a good idea if you have only a few transparencies. In that case, the frames have these advantages:

- The frame provides an opaque edge that allows only the transparency itself to project onto the screen. Otherwise, there would be a glaring edge because the face of the overhead projector is larger than a transparency.

- The frame makes handling transparencies easier.

- It takes care of the static electricity problem. Freshly prepared transparencies have an amazing amount of static electricity. That causes them to cling, turning neat stacks into messes. A frame solves the problem.

- It helps you put the transparency on straight.

I use a neat device that replaces the cardboard frames—a plastic and glass frame that sits on the face of the overhead projector.

It's like an in-box with glass on the bottom and works perfectly. The sides of the device are about half an inch tall. I simply put it on the overhead at the beginning of my presentation and worry no more.

If you don't use frames, put tape on the face of the projector to cut out the glare. Simply put a test transparency on the projector, make sure it's projecting straight on the screen, and put tape all around the outside edges of the transparency.

In effect, you create on the projector a rectangular frame made of tape.

Tip

_____

If you do use tape, don't use MASKING *tape. Use* DRAFTING *tape, which isn't very sticky. Masking tape can ruin the face of the projector: the top of the tape peels off later, but the glue tends to stay put.*

_____

If you have a lot of transparencies and use them frequently, you probably want to avoid frames. They're quite bulky. I can easily fit all the transparencies for a two-day seminar in my briefcase.

But if they had frames, I'd need several briefcases.

Tip

_____

You can write brief notes on the frame. Some people like to write their transition statements on the frame so they can read those words as they place the transparency on the projector. Others like to list a few points they want to be sure to cover. Don't put too many notes on the frame, though, or you'll have more eye contact there than with your audience.

_____

Label your transparencies

When you're giving your presentation and look down at your stack of transparencies, you can't see what's on the next one. Because they're "transparent," you can see through several at once—a jumbled mess of words and graphics.

I suggest you write a brief title on the frame for each one. I don't number my transparencies because I'm always adding another, taking one out, or rearranging. Simple titles are effective.

If you don't have frames, put a label (the kind for file folders) on the bottom corner (which often doesn't project on the screen).

Here's an example of what I mean:

The next chapter gives you further tips for designing visual aids.

CHAPTER 23

Designing visual aids
—further tips

Bottom line

As with the previous chapter, simply having visual aids is a good start, but having <u>well-designed</u> visual aids can make all the difference.

This chapter continues the previous chapter, "Designing visual aids."

These are the suggestions I'll cover:

- Be consistent with your design.
- Use varying type styles and sizes.
- Try replacing words with an image.
- Consider using graphs.
- Use only relevant clip art.

Now let's look at examples of each.

Be consistent with your design

A common mistake people make is designing good *individual* visual aids but not a good *set* of visual aids. Each may look nice, but together they don't have a uniform appearance. These three transparencies are inconsistent:

<u>PAGEFITTING</u>

PLACING THE TEXT ON THE PAGE

CHANGING THE TEXT TO FIT

Stylizing

external
internal

Sourcing

 checking facts
 checking MORE facts

Now let's use a consistent design:

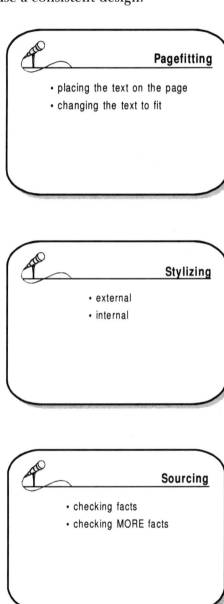

A consistent design looks good to the audience. So try to keep the titles in the consistent places on each transparency; the spacing consistent; and the typefaces consistent for titles, headings, and body text.

There's a benefit to you, too: if you (and your company) have a consistent design, you can interchange transparencies for different presentations, and for different presenters, too.

Use varying type styles and sizes

Computers give us easy access to varying type styles (such as bold and italic) and sizes.

Here's a transparency that looks decent, but it makes the common mistake of using a bold typeface for all the text:

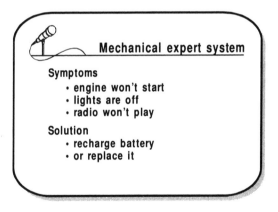

In the next chapter, I'll suggest using bold all the time for computer presentations: the lower resolution of the computer projection systems pretty well demands that. But for transparencies, bold all the time looks too bold.

Notice that you can now easily see which are the subordinate parts:

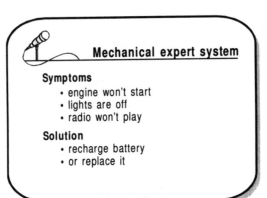

Using bold selectively helps audiences see your transparency's organization.

Try replacing words with an image

Bonnie Franklin, an expert communicator, says that the key to good visual aids is "to get the right image for the idea."

That means looking beyond using only words on a visual aid and considering a diagram, drawing, map, or other image that may communicate more efficiently.

This is the most important change taking place today with visual aids. Many business people know how to use a graphics program. So getting or designing images is usually a snap.

The result is that audiences no longer need to yawn at seeing one bullet slide after another. So let's look at some examples.

Here's a transparency that tries to describe a computer network using only words:

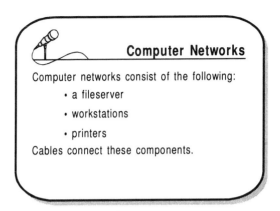

Notice how much more effective a diagram is:

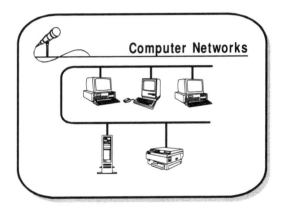

That's simple enough. What are some other types of "images"?

A drawing can be effective, too.

For example, if you're talking about something complicated like the effects of lift, drag, thrust, and gravity on an airplane, this line drawing is going to be much more effective than a word chart could ever be:

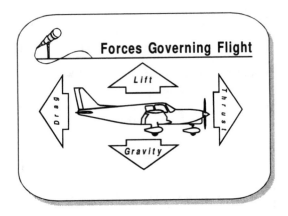

An actual picture of an airplane wouldn't work as well because it would have too many distracting features.

But a picture would be terrific for showing a building you're planning to move into, a television you're marketing, or the mountain you've just climbed.

Let's consider another example using something other than words. If you want to tell people where your regional headquarters are, your immediate thought might be to use a simple bullet transparency, like this:

But notice how much more effective a map is:

Finding the right image isn't always easy, but once you discover it, it can get across instantly what a word chart might never convey effectively at all.

Consider also using:

- process diagrams
- organization charts
- tables (not exciting but often quite helpful)
- simple cartoons
- even photographs

Consider using graphs

A graph is another kind of image that can replace words, and we're all familiar with their value. The question I'll deal with is how to present graphs so they're easier to read. Today's technology can take us beyond yesterday's traditional presentation, and a simple, efficient graph like this is easy to produce—even on word processing programs:

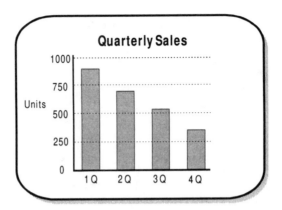

A couple of suggestions I have are to remove clutter when possible and make the title convey the bottom line. Here's one possibility:

Use only relevant clip art

Clip art is prefabricated line drawings. People can buy hundreds or even thousands of clip art images and then scatter them throughout their transparencies. Audiences naturally turn their attention first to the clip art.

That's all right if the clip art is an integral part of the transparency's content—such as the illustration of a computer network or the aerodynamic forces on an airplane.

Often, though, the clip art is no more than empty—and distracting—decoration:

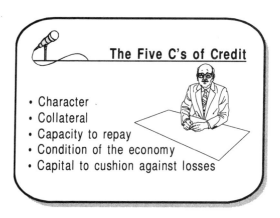

Audiences may spend time admiring your clip art rather than listening to you.

There are two good places for creative clip art, however.

One is a repeated design—on a series of transparencies in a row. If, for example, you're talking about trucks for a few transparencies, then airplanes, then trains, consider putting the image of a truck or an airplane or a train on the all the appropriate ones. That way, the clip art serves to help members of the audience recognize changes in topic (truck to airplane to train).

Another good place for creative clip art is the title transparency. It's often on the screen as the audience arrives. Because the presentation hasn't even started, the clip art can serve as an indicator that your presentation is going to be interesting.

Here's an example of clip art on a title transparency:

❖   ❖   ❖

Now let's turn to a specific application for many of these tips: computer presentations. They are the next generation of visual aids.

CHAPTER 24

Designing
computer presentations

Bottom line

*Computer presentations should be more than simply slides that
computers help project. To be fully effective, computer presentations should take advantage of the added capability and features
of computers.*

For years I used color transparencies as my primary medium when giving presentations. Now I've shifted much of
what I present to computer presentations.

That's because computer presentations allow me to use
movement, sound, and far more images to help me make
my points.

There are some drawbacks of computer presentations, such
as added equipment and expense. But the benefits usually
outweigh them as long as you're not simply showing com-
puterized overhead transparencies.

Do the last two chapters still apply for computer presentations? Absolutely! Virtually *everything* in those chapters ap-
plies fully. This chapter gives you other considerations.

Here's what I suggest:

• Consider how you'll be projecting your images.

• Be careful in choosing your fonts.

- Use more images to make your point.

- Use special effects purposefully.

Let's look at these more closely.

Consider how you'll be projecting your images

There are several ways to let audiences see what's on your computer screen:

- *Monitors.* You can project onto a large (perhaps really large) monitor. Normally, this monitor will be on a stand in front of an audience. But there could be several monitors, and they could be hanging from the ceiling.

- *Televisions.* You can use little gizmos to hook your computer into a regular television. The resolution isn't as good as with a monitor, but it's workable with small audiences.

- *LCD panels.* These are "liquid crystal display" panels and are quite popular. They sit on top of overhead projectors. The light passes through the panel and projects the image onto the same kind of screen you'd use for projecting an ordinary transparency. You want to be sure you have a very bright overhead projector; otherwise, the audience will see a dim image on the screen.

- *Projectors.* These look a little like 35-millimeter slide projectors. They sit on a table or hang from the ceiling. And although they're heavy and expensive, they project the brightest image.

So why is it important for you to know how you'll be projecting your image? Well, there are some design considerations.

For example, if you're using an LCD panel, the lights will probably have to be very dim in the room. There is a good chance you'll seem like a disembodied voice. So if there are parts when you expect the audience members to be looking at you, they may not be able to see you easily. Therefore, you need to design your presentation to show more on the screen.

Also, if you're using a monitor or television, using a pointer can be quite awkward. Don't count on it. Let images on the screen (like suddenly appearing arrows) show your audience where to look.

And images on a monitor or television may be quite a bit smaller than those you'd have with an LCD panel. As a result, fonts and graphics need to be bigger with a monitor or television.

Tip

Regardless of how you project your image, try to use a remote mouse. You can move about the room easily and simply click whenever you want the next image to come on the screen.

Be careful in choosing your fonts

In Chapter 22, I recommended 28-point sans serif type for transparencies, and I said you should use bold only for titles. However, for computer presentations, I want to modify that recommendation.

The resolution for computer presentations is normally not as good as for transparencies. For computer presentations, then, I recommend at least 32 points for your text, bold all the time. Sans serif type is even more important for computer presentations, again because it projects better when your medium has poorer resolution.

The size may need to be even larger than 32 points. You may want to experiment with 34-point or even 36-point type.

Since you're using such a large point size, you may want to use a condensed font, such as Arial Narrow, to get more on the page. You can see that Arial Narrow takes less horizontal space than Arial, but still looks large on the page:

Arial

Arial Narrow

Both are 32-point bold—what I recommend as a minimum for your computer presentations.

You may wonder, if you are making everything bold, how to emphasize words. Color. Bright red shows up great!

Use more images to make your point

When you're using *transparencies*, you constantly need to direct your audience's attention from the screen and back to you. But with *computer presentations*, you probably want to keep your audience's attention on the screen almost all the time. Partly that's because they may not be able to see you in a dark or dimly lit room. And partly that's because there can be a lot of "action" on the screen.

The fact that the audience can't see you isn't necessarily a real problem with computer presentations: you can fire a lot of images quickly at an audience—with just a click of the mouse. In a way, a computer presentation can be like a live, narrated television show—in the most positive sense.

Let's consider an example of how to use more images. Suppose you want to teach what passive voice is. With a computer presentation, you can start by showing this image:

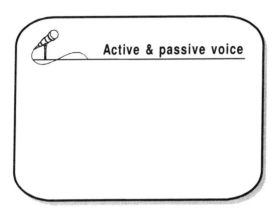

Then you can say, "So let's talk about active and passive voice. What are they? Well, here's an active sentence." Click the mouse button. An instant image:

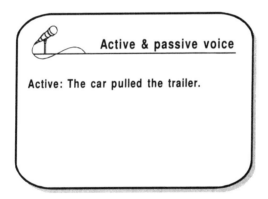

Now you can say, "What would the passive sentence be?" Click. An instant image:

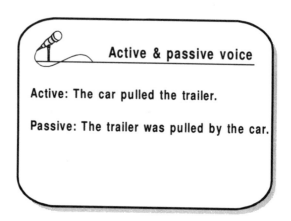

Active & passive voice

Active: The car pulled the trailer.

Passive: The trailer was pulled by the car.

"Now let's look at the active sentence. What's the subject?" The word "subject" appears instantly in red type above the word "car."

"And what's the verb?" The word "verb" appears instantly in red above the word "pulled."

All this happens fast, almost instantly, and seamlessly to the audience. You could do the same with transparencies, but the shuffling required would take more time and surely be distracting. You could do it with 35-millimeter slides, but, again, the time would be longer, and the clicking of the projector would be distracting.

Consider another example: graphs and charts. Suppose you want to show your company's profits, using a bar chart. Instead of showing the entire bar chart at once, you could show the elements—one image at a time—in this order:

- the title of the bar chart (so you can announce your topic—and give the bottom line)

- the grid (so you can explain what the numbers mean)

- the bar for the first quarter

- then the bar for the second quarter, etc.

See what you're doing? You're focusing your audience's attention, just where you want it, image after image.

The next section shows another way to do that.

Use special effects purposefully

Computer presentations can show movement, even videos, on the screen. What I want to talk about in this section is the use of transition effects.

First, what are they? You see them on television all the time. For example, the weather reporter may have the map appear to roll up or down the screen. Or a bar may move across the screen, pushing one image off the screen and another onto it.

These transition effects (or ones like them) are easy to do with computer presentations. The question is what ones to use and when to use them.

Some advice:

- *Use fancy ones to move to your title slide.* For example, start with an opaque slide, then have that slide dissolve dramatically into your title slide. This effect will draw your audience's attention just where you want it.

- *Use a fairly strong transition effect as you move to each new section of your presentation.* Use the same effect each time. This will reinforce the structure of your presentation.

- *Use transition effects sparingly elsewhere in your presentation.* If you're not reinforcing something with your effect, you're probably distracting your audience.

- *Finish with flair.* One possibility is to use a "box in" transition effect to an opaque screen. This makes your presentation seem to disappear into infinity! It's a strong finishing effect.

✛   ✛   ✛

We've looked at lots of tips for creating good visual aids. They help deliver your message and add pizzazz to your presentation. But there's a way to reinforce your message even further and keep your audience's attention: involve them. That's the subject for the next chapter.

CHAPTER 25

Involving your audience and using humor

Bottom line

Many top-notch speakers—even in formal situations—use techniques to involve their audiences. Some techniques simply move audiences from a passive to an active thinking mode; others actually get them out of their seats.

Too many presentations seem to have an invisible separator between speakers and audiences. It's like a glass wall: the speakers stay on their side and do the talking; the audiences stay on their side and do the listening. (Theater people call that the "fourth wall.")

Good speakers usually try to eliminate that wall. One way is to let the audience participate during the presentation—people love to be part of the action. Another is to get them to laugh so they will feel greater rapport with the speaker. Either way breaks down the artificial separation that usually does more harm than good.

Let's start with involving the audience.

Involving the audience

There are various degrees of involving the audience. Some speakers have the audience members actually on their feet and moving around. Others speakers simply ask for them to participate passively. Not all ways are appropriate for all presentations, but audiences are usually more willing to be active than inexperienced speakers assume.

We'll begin with the simplest way of making the audience more attentive.

Ask questions

Real questions invite audience participation. Unreal questions don't. An unreal question is when a speaker says something with a question mark at the end but doesn't pause for an answer: "Have any of you been to California recently? Well, I have. In fact . . ." There's nothing wrong with an unreal question; it just doesn't create audience participation.

But a real question does. Here are some examples:

- An accountant, speaking on technical matters relating to income tax, started with a quiz. This was one of her questions: "Suppose my sister decides to separate from her husband, so she throws the bum out on July 4th. Which filing status can she use?" She gave us three choices—and we each had to choose one. I thought that was an excellent use of the question. If she'd started, instead, with a dry listing of filing statuses and the requirements for each, the audience would surely have moved deeply into the passive mode.

- An appliance salesman asked how many people in the audience owned microwave ovens. He counted the hands and then compared the result with the national average. This was an interesting way of telling us what could have been a dry statistic: 70% of the population owns microwaves.

- A writing consultant started his seminar by asking members of the audience what they thought of the writing in their in-boxes. He went around the room, getting a response from everyone. That way, he found out what the audience members were thinking and got them actively involved in his topic.

Notice these were all questions the audience could actually answer—often easily. When you ask questions—real ones—the glass wall disappears almost immediately.

Tip

Be sure to focus your questions. One speaker held out a 20-year-old swimming fin, asking a person in the audience to touch it and give her reaction. He asked, "What do you notice about this?" She said, "It seems flexible." Unfortunately, he'd intended for her to notice how heavy it was. He should have asked, "Does this seem heavy to you?"

Use the names of people in the audience

If you refer directly to people in the audience, you show you're willing for the glass wall to come down. If you know someone, try to single that person out: "I was impressed by Betsy's work on the reorganization committee. It will dramatically improve our company's . . ." This creates a more informal atmosphere.

You can also use real people's names in scenarios you're creating. One speaker told a group about customer service representatives for a telephone company—and when they must refer questions to a supervisor. Here's how she used the name of a member of the audience: "Poor Gene. The phone truck ran over his cat and killed it. He's calling me, a customer service rep, to complain. That's one I'd refer to my supervisor." Gene (who didn't even have a cat and was a simple prop) certainly straightened up at that point.

Later in the presentation, the speaker used the name of another person in the audience. This time she explained a telephone feature (Caller ID) that lets us know who is calling before we pick up the phone: "Remember Gera's first boyfriend? She was waiting by the phone, just hoping he'd call. She wanted to sound just right when the call came. Wouldn't Caller ID have been nice for her to have had?"

You can see that simply using real people's names can brighten up the audience. Gene and Gera—unaware they'd be named in the fictitious situations—took notice. And so did the rest of the audience, everybody glancing at the person the speaker referred to.

The speaker had another nice technique: as she spoke the person's name, she walked over and looked into the person's eyes.

Tip

Mention the names of earlier speakers—that shows you can be spontaneous. For example, in a session on buying houses, a real estate agent mentioned the name of a well-known lawyer who had just spoken: "Let's say you've just gotten good legal advice from Jeannette. Now you're ready for final negotiations with the seller. Let me offer you a good strategy."

Set up tasks

You can also involve people in more active ways in your presentation. I've seen speakers ask everyone in the audience to do these:

- Write our names with our non-preferred hand (to show the strength of preferences).

- Communicate a sentence in sign language.

- Scrub for a medical operation (with pretend soap and water)—the procedure is amazingly thorough and complex.

- Do a breathing exercise designed to relieve stress (the speaker, in particular, benefited from this one).

Do these sound like they're not appropriate for business situations? For some situations, they're not. But business is exceptionally diverse, and these speakers were very successful.

Use members of the audience to demonstrate

A demonstration involving volunteers really gets the audience's collective cardiovascular system going: those participating are fully alert; those not participating are still calming down from possibly being up front themselves; and everybody enjoys the action.

Tip

> *How do you get somebody to volunteer? In some cases, ask for help in advance. Often that's not possible. So just wait quietly and look at the audience. Someone always volunteers!*

Here are some demonstrations I've seen:

- *Topic:* how to deal with an attack by muggers. The speaker had two volunteers demonstrate a mugging, one as the mugger, one as the victim. But first she explained what would happen, making especially sure the victim wouldn't overreact at being "attacked." This demonstration was extremely effective. Everyone could feel the violation of a personal attack.

- *Topic:* setting priorities. The speaker gave two members five seconds to grab as many poker chips as possible from a table. He later explained that the chips had different values: the blue were worth the most, then the red, then the white. The volunteers had to count the value of the chips they'd grabbed. The speaker then said that priorities at work have different values, too, and too often managers are so caught up in white-chip activities that they never get to the red-chip and blue-chip ones.

- *Topic:* easy ways to seal bottles. The speaker had a volunteer come forward and, using a simple device, put a cap *on* a bottle. This made the point clearly that the device was easy to use.

You can see the value of these exercises. The chairman of the board might not use them when talking to stockholders. But most presentations have the opportunity for some type of audience participation—from a relatively passive question to an active demonstration. Look for opportunities. They're often a presentation's highlight.

Tip

Be very, very sure you NEVER embarrass or trick your volunteers. They won't like it—and the audience won't either. And offer your thanks as the volunteers take their seats.

Using humor

Everybody likes humor. But not everybody agrees what's funny.

I've spoken many times when audience members filled out critique forms at the end. Early in my speaking career, I used to be surprised that jokes I felt were totally inoffensive had offended someone.

Soon I realized that the best humor is often unplanned—the little asides that happen spontaneously during a presentation, the kind that aren't necessarily funny in the cold light of day but that provoke laughter during the heightened atmosphere of a presentation.

Other types of humor have their places. Let me give you a couple of examples.

A sailor recently gave an extremely funny presentation, defining nautical terms for non-sailors. I jotted down one of his comments: "If you're on my boat, don't say there's something on the *bow* of the boat. Just say there's something hanging off the *pointy end*—looks like a person. I'll know what you mean."

He then told us some of the most important "nautical terms" non-sailors need to know. This was his visual aid:

> ### Nautical Terms To Know
>
> - "Let go of ____ !" (*this, that, them,* etc.)
>
> - "Pull this (or that)!"
>
> - "DUCK!!!!" (most important term)

This is inoffensive humor that everyone can (and did) enjoy.

Tip

If you expect to be nervous at the beginning of a presentation, avoid starting with narrative jokes. They require you to be at your best, and your timing must be perfect.

Sometimes a standard joke can work well, too. But usually the speaker should use himself as the "victim." For example, at a very large conference, the keynote speaker (a man at the top of his profession) started with this story:

> This morning, a woman came up to me and began a polite conversation:
>
> "Are you the speaker for today?" she asked.
>
> "Why, yes," I replied.
>
> "You must be quite nervous," she continued.
>
> "Well, not really. Why do you ask?" I said.
>
> "Then why else are you in the Ladies Room?"

Tip

Make yourself the target of humor. Nobody is going to be offended if you're the target, and jokes on yourself don't diminish your stature.

Humor spices up a presentation. Some you can plan; some just happens when you're especially alert and simply enjoying being the speaker.

As you can see, you can reinforce your message and add pizzazz by involving your audience and using humor. In fact, you should actually design these features into your presentation.

Once the design of your presentation is complete, you're ready to test it. That's what the next chapter is about.

CHAPTER 26

Rehearsing

Bottom line

You need to rehearse two ways: by yourself, to help remember the words you want to say; and in front of others, to be sure the words are good ones.

People who design cars wouldn't dream of trying to sell them without testing them first. People who design airplanes wouldn't think of putting passengers on them without testing them first. People acting in plays wouldn't appear on opening night without a number of rehearsals.

But people who design presentations—or prepare them, at least—often run the first test in front of their real audience. That's not the time to find out the car won't start or the plane can't get off the ground or the five-act play won't reach the end of Act I.

Rehearsal is a crucial part of preparing. Good speakers have usually said the words and tried the visual aids many times before standing up for real.

Rehearsing by yourself

You'll probably want your first rehearsal to take place by yourself. Simply go into a room that has the necessary equipment. Then give your presentation out loud (not just in your mind) to the wall and chairs. Again, again, and again.

When my daughter was young, she loved the *Little House on the Prairie* series of books. I once saw her finish a book and turn right to page one and start again. That's like what I do when I rehearse a new presentation.

Tip

> *Especially rehearse the beginning and the end of your presentation—the moments of greatest impact.*

One reason I rehearse is to find the words. My feeling is that if I can find the right words once, they'll come to mind more easily the next time. And the next. To me, that's much more effective than memorizing.

That reminds me of a line in E. B. White's famous essay, "Once More to the Lake." In it, White describes returning to his childhood vacation place decades later. He says, "It is strange how much you can remember about places like that *once you allow your mind to return into the grooves that lead back.*"

I think of rehearsing as making those grooves, of getting the words right, not so I can return to them decades later—but just a few days later. That way, when the ideas come to me, the words will, too.

Tip

> *If possible, rehearse at least once in the room you'll actually use for your presentation. You'll feel more like the room is "yours." Also, you'll find out about lighting, the on/off switch for the overhead projector, etc.*

When you rehearse, be sure to actually use your visual aids. You'll get practice introducing them properly and handling them. Just as important, you'll find out which ones don't project well and need work.

Rehearsing in front of others

Rehearsing by yourself helps you get the words right, but it doesn't really test your presentation. For that, you need other people. Unfortunately, the speakers who most need a live test audience are the ones least likely to ask for one. In fact, some speakers are more self-conscious rehearsing in front of a handful of co-workers than giving the presentation to the real audience.

Once you break through that self-consciousness, though, you'll find this is the most important way of all to rehearse. You'll find out what works and doesn't work with everything about your presentation—from the organization to the content to the visual aids to the audience involvement. The changes you make as a result will often be invaluable.

I suggest you try to get people to hear you who may be typical of your real audience. That way, you'll be running a true test.

When you do rehearse in front of other people, ask them not to interrupt you the first time through—to take notes, instead. Otherwise, you'll be getting constant interruptions. Both you and your test audience will lose the flow of your presentation.

Tip

Have someone time your rehearsal. Audiences get restless if you go over your allotted time. And you'll get nervous if you fall way short.

In addition, I try to rehearse at least once in front of my wife. Other people tell me their spouses give pretty straightforward criticism, too.

Rehearsing in front of a camera

Many companies have videotape equipment. If they don't, you possibly may have a video camera at home. Videotaping doesn't show you much about the organization or content of your presentation, but it does reveal a lot about your techniques of delivery: Are you pacing too much? Jittery? Saying "uh" or "okay"?

You don't need to videotape yourself more than once, but that once can let *you* see what your *audience* will surely see. And seeing it for yourself is much more effective than having other people tell you.

Tip

When you're being videotaped, be sure the camera stays on you—not on the screen showing your visual aids. The intent is to videotape YOU, *not your presentation.*

The next part of the book offers suggestions on how to give your presentation, covering such topics as setting up the room, presenting your visual aids, and using effective techniques of delivery. You'll want to read that part before you actually begin rehearsing.

Appendix B, "Checklist for speakers," gives you reminders of what makes for a good presentation. You might want your test audience to have this checklist during your rehearsal.

GIVING YOUR
PRESENTATION

CHAPTER 27

Setting up the room

Bottom line

Many things can be wrong with the room you give your presentation in, and any one of them can cause your presentation to fail.

Even if your presentation is well designed and rehearsed, it may not succeed if the room isn't right. Little things— like a few extra degrees of temperature—can create a negative environment that makes listening almost impossible.

This chapter will cover what I look for in a room. I've learned most of this from hard experience. Here is what I check:

- the projector and screen
- the tables and chairs
- the microphone
- the lighting
- the temperature
- outside distractions

You may think an audiovisual crew (if there is one) should have all these ready, but from my experience, they don't. They arrange things from their perspective, but not from the perspective of an experienced speaker. Out of about a hundred presentations I give a year, the room is nearly right only a handful of times.

You may also think you don't have control of the room. Sometimes that's true. But most people have more control than they think. Get there early, let people know what you need, and they'll almost always be accommodating. The effort can make all the difference.

So let's look more closely now at these factors, and I'll give you some practical suggestions for each.

Checking the projector and screen

I can't rest until I know the audience can see my visual aids, so I go straight for the overhead projector. If I'm speaking in a hotel and get there the night before, I ask someone to open the room for me right then so I can check that projector. Otherwise, I won't be able to sleep.

This is what I look for:

- *Does the projector focus well?* Sometimes a projector focuses on part of the screen but not the rest. If that's the case, look for a lever to adjust the focal length. If there isn't one, you'll want to get another projector.

  If that isn't possible, try to get the best focus at the *top* of the screen and work as much as possible there. If you've designed your transparencies so most of the content is at the top, you'll at least make the best of a bad situation.

  By the way, I use a test transparency (see Chapter 22) for checking the overhead projector.

- *Is there a spare bulb—and does it work?* Normally turn off the projector before moving the lever on it to the spare bulb. And try to slide the lever smoothly so you don't break the filament in the good bulb. Sometimes the spare is brighter than the original. In that case, use the spare.

- *When the transparency is straight on the face of the projector, does it project straight on the screen?* Projectors are hard to line up with screens, and they get hard use, too (things get bent). Often what looks straight on the face of the projector is quite crooked on the screen.

Sometimes you can move the projector left or right and get a different angle for the projection. That may solve the problem. If not, experiment until you find what angle you should use for placing the transparency on the projector, and remember that angle.

- *Is the projected image large enough for the audience to see?* Go to the far corners of the room and look at your projected image. If you have good eyesight, make allowances for those who don't.

If the image is too small, move the projector and screen farther apart so the projected image fills the screen as much as possible. If the image is still too small, consider rearranging the audience's tables and chairs (more later on that). Or try to get a larger screen.

- *Is the extension cord from the projector a hazard?* Because I can trip over anything, I try to avoid setting traps for myself. I normally stand with the projector on my right side as I face the audience, so I want the extension cord to run to an outlet even farther to the right. (Left-handed people should adjust accordingly.)

I don't want the cord to run across any path I'll normally take during my presentation, except for occasional movements to the other side of the room.

- *Is the overhead projector on an adequate table?* I try to avoid stands designed just for overhead projectors. Usually they hold the projector and nothing else. I won't have room for my transparencies, and I need room not only for the stack of transparencies I'm going to use but also for the stack I've already used. The stands are also sometimes high, blocking the view of some members of the audience.

  I try to find a moderately low table that has room for the projector and two stacks of transparencies. I leave room on the left side of the table (as I face the audience) for both stacks of my transparencies. I then set up the projector on the right side of the table.

Checking the tables and chairs

Once you have the equipment set up for your visual aids, you have to turn your attention to the seating for the audience. You usually don't have any control over the comfort of the chairs or the steadiness of the tables, but you probably do have control over their position.

- *Can the audience see all right?* If the seating is very close to the screen and very wide from left to right, people on the edges may not be able to see the screen. Their angle will be too shallow.

  If the seating goes too far back, people in the back may not be able to see. If necessary, rearrange the room (that's how I stay in shape). The local staff is normally quite helpful.

- *Can you move freely?* If you're like me, you want to move all around the room. For a small audience, I like the seating to be in the shape of a "U" with my table and projector filling part of the opening. Then I can move inside or outside the "U" as I speak.

Checking the microphone

A microphone is a great benefit if you have a large audience. If you're in the marginal area where you think the audience can "probably" hear you without one, ask for one anyway. Otherwise, you'll end up raising your voice unnaturally: that will strain your vocal cords (so you'll be hoarse the rest of the day); also, an unnaturally loud voice is hard for your audience to listen to—your natural inflection disappears.

You want a wireless microphone if at all possible. That way you can move freely to the projector, the screen, and the audience. A microphone with a wire is all right, but once again, that's a hazard for those of us who are clumsy.

Try to stay away from a fixed microphone—one that's part of a lectern. You'll be as immobile as the lectern.

If you are using a microphone, this is what you should check:

- *Is the volume adjusted correctly?* Talk over the microphone and have someone walk to all parts of the room to check the volume. When you talk, try to speak with the same loudness you expect to have during your presentation. In my case, I tend to speak just a bit louder than normal during a presentation, so I speak with a little extra loudness during the test, too. By the way, as I test the microphone, I simply recite the alphabet.

- *Does it make unwanted noises?* I'm no electrical engineer, but audiovisual people tell me that a wireless mike needs a new battery very often. In fact, they'll normally replace the battery more than once a day during constant use. So if you hear a scratchy noise or static, have a new battery put in. If the microphone makes high-pitched squeals, lower the volume.

- *Can you turn your head to the side and still project?* Microphones have different designs. Some pick up your voice very well no matter how much you swivel your head from side to side. Others don't. This matters when you're turning your head toward the screen and talking at the same time: the microphone stays put, but the position of your mouth relative to it doesn't.

Tip

Don't put a lapel microphone on your lapel. It will be too far to one side or the other and sometimes not pick up your voice well. Instead, fasten it to your tie (for men) or to your blouse (for women).

- *Does it have a fastener that works?* Like projectors, microphones get hard use. And the fasteners for lapel mikes are often fragile. You don't want to find out there's a problem just as you're being introduced.

Tip

For women: Be careful of necklaces when you use a lapel microphone—sometimes they bang against it and make scraping or jangling noises.

Checking the lighting

You don't want a dark room. The lighting that makes your transparencies look perfectly beautiful is too dark. Your audience will begin to hibernate. Set the lights as bright as you can so the audience can still see the transparencies pretty well.

If you're using 35-millimeter slides or a computer presentation, you may need the lights lower than for transparencies. In that case, have someone lower the lights just when you use your visual aids. And have someone turn the lights back up when you're through with them.

Also, you don't want a light directly over your screen: it will shine on the screen and wash out your projected transparencies. If possible, move the screen a little so the light is behind it. If that won't work . . . well, I've had a lot of experience unscrewing light bulbs. Just get a steady chair.

Ideally, you want less light over the screen and nearly normal light elsewhere.

Checking the temperature

A warm room is a sleepy room. You want the temperature a little on the cool side when the audience is in the room. That means the room should be even cooler when it is empty. If the temperature seems just right when you're setting up, it will probably be too warm once everyone gets there.

Checking for outside distractions

Muzak. It sounds so nice you don't even notice it when you're setting up. But it becomes immediately obvious when the audience settles down and introductions begin.

Another problem is the open door. You can't keep the door closed forever (the audience *will* come in). But if you hear outside noises even slightly during your presentation, the people sitting near the door are probably very distracted. Just ask someone to close it. People in the audience are usually glad to help.

✛   ✛   ✛

Once you've set up rooms a few times, you'll learn what to look for. And when the room is the way you like it, you'll sense that it's *yours*. That helps you feel confident when the presentation begins.

Appendix C is a checklist for setting up the room.

CHAPTER 28

Using effective techniques of delivery

Bottom line

Once you have a well-designed and well-rehearsed presentation, many techniques of delivery take care of themselves. Still, there are some important things to watch for in your rehearsal and in your final delivery.

Now your preparation is over, and you're ready for the actual presentation.

This is when speakers get nervous. Even though I've spoken many times, I occasionally feel the butterflies before an important presentation in front of a lot of people. That's natural. To calm myself down, I don't do yoga or deep breathing exercises. I simply look over my visual aids and review what I'm going to say for each one. Quickly I realize: "Oh, this is easy! I can do this!" I know my material, and the design and rehearsal have prepared me to present it.

I also try to think of my presentation as a conversation with my audience. I'll be the only one speaking much of the time, but, still, I'm just talking to them. Yes, I'll project more energy and have better focus, but I'll just be having a friendly conversation.

There are some techniques that can make that friendly conversation more effective. Here's what I recommend:

- start fast
- project energy
- move around the room
- make eye contact
- speak with good loudness and pace
- avoid distractions

Start fast

Most audiences decide pretty quickly whether they want to listen to you or not. Yet speakers who have great visual aids and a nice presentation sometimes ramble at the beginning—the time they haven't yet showed the audience their first visual aid.

The solution? Say the minimum and get to your first visual aid.

If you've designed your presentation well, it may be a funny quotation or something else that will quickly engage your audience.

An efficient start needn't seem abrupt to your audience. More likely, it will just seem like you're well prepared.

Tip

Here's a trick many speakers use to feel comfortable at the start: find a friendly face and talk to that person. You can create that friendly face by talking to members of the audience beforehand—especially if you're in the room as they come in. Then look at that person at the beginning of your presentation. As you gain confidence, look around. You should start finding more friendly faces there, too.

Project energy

Projecting energy doesn't necessarily mean moving frenetically. It simply means showing—through your posture, your movement, your facial expression, your voice—that you *care* about what you're saying. If you don't show that you care, how can you expect your audience to?

Sometimes, especially during a long presentation, you have to give yourself a pep talk, tell yourself to pick up your energy a notch. When you do, you'll almost invariably get the same response from your audience.

Projecting energy, by the way, doesn't mean that you have to do anything out of the ordinary. Just act within your own personality: how do you behave when you really care about something? That's how you should behave during your presentation.

People who lack confidence in themselves are sometimes reluctant to project energy. They try to blend in with the wall. As a result, they fulfill their own expectations: they don't do as well as they should. So if you're not used to projecting energy in front of others, take a chance. You'll see the benefits immediately.

Move around the room

Someone is in control of the room. Either the speaker is or the audience is. When the audience is in control, speakers feel that the only space they own is where they're standing. When the speaker is in control of the room, audience members feel the only space they own is where they're sitting.

That sounds like a fight for control, doesn't it? But it really isn't. *Everyone* wants the speaker to be in control of the room. One of the best ways to show that control is to move.

Movement is good for two other reasons:

- *It helps the audience.* Imagine people in the audience with their heads and necks in the same position for an entire presentation. That would be extremely uncomfortable, wouldn't it? But if you move around the room, you're giving them different angles, slightly different body positions, for viewing you.

- *It helps you.* Now imagine just standing in one place for your entire presentation. Could you stay there if you weren't giving a presentation? If so, what would the physical consequences be? Stiff legs, stiff back, stiff neck. So moving actually helps relax you as you speak.

Although movement is helpful, even crucial at times, I have seen successful presentations without it.

I attended a presentation in an auditorium that held about 400 senior government executives. The speaker was sitting in a big easy chair on the stage. The audience was used to that: speakers always sat there during introductions.

The introduction took place, and the speaker never moved. He just sat there! The audience didn't know how to react because that had never happened before.

Then the person in the chair started speaking. He was energetic. He leaned forward and fixed the audience with his eyes. Contrary to what we'd expect from someone just sitting in an easy chair, he was full of energy.

He didn't move around the room, but he took control in another way: he stayed in his chair. He did the unexpected. And he did everything else right.

His delivery was so terrific that he didn't need to move around the room. He projected plenty of energy from where he was.

Tip

People wonder what to do with their hands while speaking. There isn't a simple answer. What do you do with them when talking to one or two people in an informal situation? That's what you should do with them when you're in front of many people. If you become conscious of your hands, don't put them in your pockets. If you're nervous, they'll just appear awkward. Instead, let them hang naturally by your sides. They won't be doing anything, but they won't be distracting, either. As you relax, your hands will naturally come alive again.

Make eye contact

Have you ever heard the suggestion to look just over the heads of the people in your audience? That's bad advice. You need to look right at them.

Imagine someone talking only to you for a few minutes without ever making eye contact: first that person looks down, then to the right, then to the left, then down again, all the while talking. That would seem pretty strange, wouldn't it? That's what happens when a speaker doesn't look at the audience. The audience starts to feel the speaker is talking *at* them, not *to* them.

Eye contact, by the way, isn't a behavior you try to acquire as a speaker. It's more a symptom—a symptom that you are actually trying to talk to people. When you're really trying to communicate, the eye contact is automatically there. It remains on an individual for at least a couple of seconds and then moves to another. It takes in all parts of the room.

Sometimes eye contact is hard when you're working at the overhead projector. The light from it is so bright that your eyes can't adjust to it and to the audience. In that case, you have to fake eye contact. You're actually "blind," but face outward and look different directions. You can still see vague shapes out there.

Tip

Don't forget to smile (unless you're giving bad news or being stern on purpose). A smile really helps break the tension. There's a saying among speakers that "the face you give is the face you get." If you see lots of frowns in the audience, check your own expression.

Speak with good loudness and pace

If you speak too quietly for people to hear, you won't communicate. That's obvious. So if you're naturally soft-spoken, move closer to the audience and ask people to let you know if they have trouble hearing. Try to get a microphone if that's at all appropriate. Soft-spoken people using a microphone often have marvelous inflection that others didn't know was there. Also, all speakers should try to speak fairly quickly. Lots of people think they speak *too* quickly. Only a few of them are right. Audiences much prefer a speaker who goes fast rather than one who goes too slow. Very slow speakers drive audiences crazy for a minute or two. Then most audiences tune them out.

Tip

Even though you should speak fairly quickly, try to still have numerous pauses for emphasis. Think of pauses as punctuation. You'd have trouble reading a book with no punctuation, wouldn't you? Similarly, audiences have trouble listening to someone speak without pauses.

Avoid distractions

If you're doing something distracting, the audience will have great difficulty paying attention to what you're saying.

You can distract people with verbal mannerisms: "uh" and "okay" are two of the most common (we've all counted other people's "uh's"). You cannot eliminate these entirely and shouldn't try. Just watch the top newscasters on television when they're not reading the news—when they're part of a round-table discussion or interviewing someone. You'll hear the "uh's," but probably not to distraction. And that's the key: keeping the verbal mannerisms under control so they don't distract your audience.

You can also distract with excessive movement. As I mentioned earlier, some movement is good and contributes to the energy of your presentation. That's purposeful movement. Movement that isn't so good is anything jittery or a noticeable pattern.

Some speakers pace back and forth, back and forth, back and . . . That drives audiences crazy. Others wave the pointer wildly or click pens. To see if you have any distracting mannerisms, ask people to note them during your rehearsals. Or, even better, note them yourself by having your rehearsal videotaped.

❖ ❖ ❖

There's another consideration for delivering your presentation: handling visual aids. There are some definite do's and don't's that can make or break it. They're the subject of the next chapter.

Appendix B, "Checklist for speakers," is a quick summary of the main points of this chapter.

CHAPTER 29

Presenting visual aids

Bottom line

Your audience should know when to look at the screen (and be able to see it) and when to look at you.

One of the most important techniques of delivery is presenting visual aids properly. That's why I've reserved an entire chapter for it. I'll concentrate on the overhead transparency—by far the most common type of visual aid. But, as I mentioned earlier, what works well for transparencies generally works well for other types of visual aids, too. The concepts are the same.

These are the two most important fundamentals in presenting visual aids:

- Don't block your audience's view.

- Direct your audience's attention where you want it.

The rest of the chapter will discuss these in more detail.

Don't block your audience's view

Usually the overhead projector is between the audience and the screen. So whenever you're standing by the projector, *you're* between the audience and the screen, too—often blocking the view. Here's an illustration:

As you can see, when you're standing by the projector, you're in the wrong place: you're blocking the view of people in front of you and on your left.

To keep out of their way, put a transparency on the projector and *then move immediately back to the screen and to the side.* Here's an illustration of the right place to stand:

This seems obvious, but many speakers—even experienced ones—stand in the wrong place. They have to be by the projector to put transparencies on and take them off.

Then they stay there—in the one place they must be during a presentation—and never move.

Tip

Be sure the area next to the screen is clear. You don't want to worry about a chair there or a table or an extension cord to trip over.

Giving your audience a clear view of the screen requires conscious effort on your part. Moving to the screen has a side benefit, too: it also moves the audience's attention there. That's what the next section is about.

Direct your audience's attention where you want it

Good speakers are conscious of directing the audience's attention. Sometimes you want members of your audience to look at the screen; other times you want them to look at you. It's up to you to help the audience look at the right place.

Most good speakers believe the audience can have its conscious attention only one place at a time. For example, if the speaker is talking and there's also a transparency projecting on the screen, what should the members of the audience do: Should they listen to the speaker? Or should they study the new transparency?

If they try to do both, they'll probably do neither. They can't pay attention to the speaker because there's a transparency on the screen. And they can't pay attention to the transparency because the speaker is talking.

So here are some suggestions for helping the audience keep its attention where you want it:

- Show the visual aid at the right time.

- Remove the visual aid at the right time.

- Cover parts of some visual aids.
- Use a pointer.
- Read most visual aids aloud.

Let's look more closely at these.

Show the visual aid at the right time

The instant you show a transparency, the audience will look at it. You can take advantage of that natural reaction by showing the transparency only when you want the audience to look at it.

Too often, though, beginning speakers confuse and distract audiences by doing things in the wrong order:

- First they show the transparency to the audience.
- Then they introduce it.
- Then they comment on it in detail.

You can see the problem—members of the audience look at the transparency while the speaker is introducing it but not talking specifically about what's on it. Their attention is divided—seeing one thing and hearing another.

My suggestion is to use this order instead:

- First, introduce the transparency (without showing it).
- *Then* show it to the audience.
- And then—immediately—comment on it in detail.

That way, the audience won't have its attention divided.

If you're handling your own transparencies, you won't have any trouble knowing what your next transparency is without showing it to the audience. Just look down at your stack of transparencies and read the label of the top one. You can tell what's next, but the audience can't. A problem can arise, though, if someone else handles your transparencies while you speak: he or she has the stack; you don't. How can you tell what your next transparency is if you can't see it? That's one good reason to handle your own transparencies.

Tip

If you have a big stack of transparencies, don't put them all on your table at once. Just put enough to last until the next break. That way the audience won't get worried about the number of transparencies remaining—and the length of time your presentation will take.

If you must have someone else handle your transparencies, keep a list of them handy as you speak. Computer programs can produce such a list easily, even showing several miniature copies of transparencies on a single page.

Remove the visual aid at the right time

So the right time to *show* the transparency is the instant you're ready for the audience to look at it. Does that mean the right time to *remove* the transparency is the instant you're through with it? Not necessarily. If the transparency is simple—perhaps containing only a few bullets—it won't be a distraction on the screen while you're introducing the next topic. Simply leave it there. By then the audience has probably seen enough of it that they're looking elsewhere for amusement.

But if the transparency is a graph or an interesting picture or a chart full of controversial data, remove it as soon as you're through. Turn off the projector if you have a long introduction to the next transparency. Or just leave the projector on (projecting only light) if your introduction is short. Some people object mightily to having a projector on without a transparency showing. They feel the bright light distracts the audience. So they turn the projector off every time they introduce a transparency. Some even turn the projector off and on every time they change a transparency.

I don't think that's a good practice for two reasons: First, all that clicking on and off certainly distracts the audience. They'll start watching the mechanics of what the speaker is doing instead of listening. And second, the bulb in the projector is much more likely to burn out when the projector is being turned on. Constantly turning the projector on and off greatly increases the chance of blowing out the bulb in the middle of your presentation.

Cover parts of some visual aids

This suggestion is controversial. Some people hate it. Some people love it. I'm in the second category—a real believer. Fairly often a speaker has a transparency with several related points on it, like this:

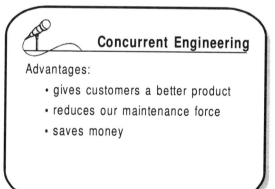

Concurrent Engineering

Advantages:
- gives customers a better product
- reduces our maintenance force
- saves money

Once the speaker introduces it and shows it on the screen, he plans to talk a little about each point. Members of the audience, however, aren't likely to look at only the first point while the speaker is talking about it. Instead, they'll naturally let their attention wander to point two, then to point three, then think a little about point two . . . All the while, the speaker is still talking about point one. The problem? The audience's attention is divided, and the speaker unintentionally provided the distraction (points two and three on the screen too early).

One solution is to have three transparencies with a point on each one. That works sometimes. But other times, the speaker wants all three on the screen at the same time. Or has only quick comments about each point and doesn't want the distraction of quickly moving transparencies on and off the projector.

In that case, cover the second and third points while talking about the first one. A sheet of paper works fine (or a system of overlays). As you finish talking about the first point, simply slide the cover down so points one and two are visible. And so forth. Here's an illustration of how I use a piece of paper to cover the second and third points while talking about the first one:

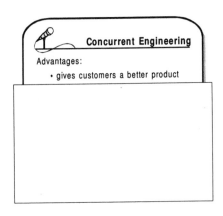

When I'm ready for point two, I simply slide the paper down:

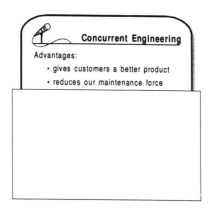

By the way, an advantage of using a piece of paper for the cover is that you can read through it when you look at the overhead projector. In other words, you can see what your next point is (so you can introduce it), but your audience can't. Another advantage of the cover is that you can write brief notes on it.

So try using a cover. You'll clearly see how powerfully you can focus your audience's attention. I use a cover constantly in all my briefings. Once you try it, you'll feel lost without that piece of paper.

If, instead of using transparencies, you're using a computer presentation, you can easily show only one bullet at a time. That's often inadvisable with transparencies, because of all the shuffling and constantly moving transparencies on and off the projector.

Use a pointer

A pointer, used correctly, is an extremely effective tool. For example, picture a speaker who only stands beside the screen and talks—without using a pointer to direct the audience's attention:

Now picture another speaker who stands beside the screen and uses a pointer each time she wants the audience to look there:

See the difference? The second speaker constantly directs the attention of members of the audience—letting them know when to look at her and when to look at the screen.

Even during a short presentation, members of the audience can relax, letting the speaker do the work of directing their attention.

The pointer has another advantage: it not only directs the attention of the audience; it also visually reinforces transitions. We've all had the experience of speakers saying, "Now for my fourth point . . ."—and we thought they were still on their first one! But the pointer unmistakably takes the audience from point one to point two, from point two to point three, and so forth.

A third advantage of using the pointer is that it creates purposeful movement for you and for your hands. You're doing something controlled and professional looking. You don't have to worry any longer about what to do with your hands during a presentation. And the pointer moves you to the screen—the right place to be.

Some people point by placing a pen on the transparency itself. However, that tends to anchor the speaker to the projector, interfering with the audience's view.

I recommend standing by the screen and using a simple wooden pointer or the metal kind that looks like a telescoping antenna. Just be watchful of fiddling with it and distracting the audience.

By the way, I suggest avoiding "laser" pointers—the kind that project a light (often an arrow) on the screen. It's somewhat difficult to hold the light steadily on one spot. As a result, the audience often sees an arrow wobbling crazily on the screen.

And there's a great temptation to move the light all over the screen while talking (the same thing can happen during computer presentations when speakers use the mouse arrow as a pointer—lots of meandering and jittery movement).

If you really want to use a laser pointer, just flash it momentarily on the screen, circle the item you want the audience to look at, and then turn it off. That gives the value of a pointer and minimizes distraction.

Tip

When you use a pointer, face the audience and hold the pointer in your hand closer to the screen. If you use the hand away from the screen, you tend to turn your body away from the audience and toward the screen. That can make you harder to hear. It can also draw you more in front of the screen so you block your audience's view.

Read most visual aids aloud

Audiences hate having speakers do nothing but read to them—no talking, no side comments, just reading one transparency after another. And I have to agree.

But there's valuable reinforcement for an audience to *see* the words on a screen and *hear* them, too. So I suggest reading every word on a transparency aloud to your audience.

Of course, as I mentioned earlier, there shouldn't be very many words on your transparency—normally just what would be the headings and sub-headings if you'd actually written down your entire speech. In other words, your "paragraphs" aren't on the transparency, just the headings and sub-headings.

Occasionally, though, you do need more than just headings and sub-headings. Perhaps you have an especially good quotation. Or a precise definition. You want the audience to comprehend every word. Again, I suggest you actually read the words aloud.

From my experience, asking members of the audience to read the words to themselves doesn't work very well. Many of them accept that as an invitation for a mental vacation.

To keep the audience from feeling "read to," however, intersperse a few comments as you're reading. For example, suppose I want to read aloud a quote from my favorite writer, E. B. White, showing how masterfully he uses simple language. This would be my transparency:

E. B. White's Girlfriend

Her name was Eileen. She was my age and she was a quiet, nice looking girl. She never came over to my yard to play, and I never went over there, and, considering that we lived so near each other, we were remarkably uncommunicative; nevertheless, she was the girl I singled out, at one point, to be of special interest to me. Being of special interest to me involved practically nothing on the girl's part—it simply meant that she was under constant surveillance. On my own part, it meant that I suffered an astonishing disintegration when I walked by her house, from embarrassment, fright, and the knowledge that I was in enchanted territory.

After the phrase "she was under constant surveillance," I'd probably say, "Remember those days?" The simple comment helps prevent the audience's perception that I'm only reading to them.

✛   ✛   ✛

So keep in mind the two fundamentals of presenting visual aids: let members of the audience see the screen and keep their attention where you want it to be.

The techniques require rehearsal but soon become automatic—just like driving a car with a stick shift.

Now let's turn our attention to the finale of your presentation: handling questions and answers.

CHAPTER 30

Handling questions and answers

Bottom line

Prepare for the Q & A session as part of your preparation for your presentation.

Sometimes there isn't a formal question-and-answer session—members of the audience ask questions throughout. That's especially good during small, informal sessions. The questions help break the invisible "glass wall" between speaker and audience. They can also help relax the speaker by turning the presentation into a conversation.

For some presentations, however, questions may be interruptions. If someone does interrupt with a question, just give a quick, polite response (including the bottom line) and explain that you'll go into more detail later.

If you do intend to have a formal question-and-answer session, you can plan for it—you needn't be totally at the mercy of your audience. You can prepare so that the unexpected becomes the exception:

- One way is to imagine the questions you'll most probably be asked and prepare for them.

- Another way is to imagine the questions you'd *hate* the audience to ask—then prepare answers for them. I've known speakers who prepare for their important presentations by brainstorming these difficult questions and answers with key members of their staff. And then rehearse answering the questions.

In either case, consider preparing visual aids to support you during the question-and-answer session. They have the same value here as they do in the regular part of your presentation.

However, even if you are confident of the content for a question-and-answer session and have some backup transparencies, there are still some techniques to consider. For the rest of the chapter, I'll cover:

- how to start the question-and-answer session

- where to stand and where to look

- how to handle difficult questioners

- how to end the session

How to start the question-and-answer session

Normally you'll finish your main presentation with a brief summary. The audience should know you're through by the content and the inflection in your voice.

To give another signal that the presentation is over, turn off the projector (or other electronic device, if you're using one) and move toward the audience. At the same time, specifically ask for questions: "That's the end of my formal presentation. I have a few minutes for questions. Does anybody have one?"

Sometimes audiences aren't immediately ready to ask questions—they simply haven't had time to think of any. If you sense there are genuine questions waiting but the audience just isn't prepared, you can ask the first question yourself: "Well, let me start. A common question is just how often . . ."

When you're through with your own (brief) answer, ask again for questions. Pause and make significant eye contact. Just wait. A question is bound to happen. The silence will grow uncomfortable, and you can wait longer than they can.

On the other hand, there's nothing wrong with no questions whatsoever. If the members of the audience really don't have any, why create artificial questions?

Where to stand and where to look

A general rule is to move closer to the audience during the question-and-answer session. That gives a subconscious signal that you're confident by showing you'll enter into the audience's space without any visual aids, notes, or other props.

In fact, if there's a stage and you have a portable microphone, consider actually leaving the stage and walking out into the audience.

If you're in a smaller room, you'll be tempted to move toward the person asking a question. That's fine unless the questioner has a soft voice. Then you're *really* tempted to move toward the questioner—but you shouldn't.

Instead, move farther away. That will usually make the questioner speak more loudly so everyone can hear. And audiences are more comfortable hearing the actual question rather than a rephrasing by the speaker.

If the audience still can't hear the question, however, be sure to repeat it for everyone before answering.

Tip

> *If you don't know the answer, say so. The audience can always tell.*

Start your answer by looking directly at the questioner. Then look outward and include the rest of the audience. Look back several times at the questioner to be sure you're answering properly. In general, spend about a third of the time looking at the questioner and two-thirds looking at the rest of the audience.

Tip

> *When you're through answering a question, normally ask the questioner if you answered it all right. If not, try again. Everybody in the audience appreciates a speaker who takes questions seriously.*

If the questioner is an important person or you especially want to be sure you've answered the question well, finish by standing near the questioner and looking at him or her.

On the other hand, if you don't want to hear from that person again, you have a couple of choices:

- finish on the far side of the room from that person
- finish right next to that person but look outward at the rest of the audience

Then ask for more questions.

How to handle difficult questioners

You don't want the audience's final impression of your presentation to be an awkward situation that developed during your question-and-answer session. Here are three types of difficult questioners and some advice on how to handle them (or try to handle them, at least):

- *The long-winded questioner.* Some people seem more interested in giving speeches than in genuinely asking for information. That's normally presumptuous of them and impolite to the rest of the audience.

  The main way to end their "speech" is to break in at the tiniest pause, pretend that was the end of their question, and resume control of the room by giving your answer. Then, of course, don't ask if you've answered their question satisfactorily and don't look their way again.

- *The incomprehensible questioner.* Sometimes it's hard to figure out what the question is. When that happens, I assume the questioner has good intentions, so I try rephrasing the question: "I'm not sure I understand your question. Are you asking . . . ?"

  Work for a minute to get on the same wavelength with the questioner. In a case like this, the audience appreciates your sincerity.

- *The hostile questioner.* Some questioners have impure motives, so there's little you can do to turn them into understanding, sympathetic friends. Your goal, normally, is to limit the damage. Answer briefly (and normally forcefully) and turn elsewhere.

  Above all, don't get "hooked"—that's when the speaker loses control and argues with the questioner. Or gets sarcastic. Or nasty. That's the surest way to lose not only your temper but the entire audience as well. Try to assume the demeanor of a calm, serious, unemotional, and well-intentioned person. Sometimes you'll have to work very hard at it.

How to end the session

The most common way to end the question-and-answer session is with a smile and a "thank you." But you can add some polish, too. A final transparency (I try to get something relevant and humorous) sends the audience out smiling and shows you've thought through your presentation. You add just a bit of formality at the end—a finishing touch.

FINAL WORDS
ON SPEAKING

CHAPTER 31

Helping others speak better

Bottom line

Help ineffective speakers by helping them <u>design</u> a good presentation—and by helping them rehearse it, too.

Perhaps you have people working for you who give presentations. Or there's a co-worker or friend who needs some help. How can you help them become better speakers?

Too often, those helping with a presentation simply look through the other person's transparencies and then offer suggestions. However, that's often too late in the process. And, because there's no rehearsal, it doesn't show what will happen when the person actually stands up.

The time for you to get involved is in the *design* stage— helping them design a presentation that will be easier to give. You should also propose a rehearsal or two.

Beginning speakers are often nervous about rehearsing in front of others. So during the first rehearsal, I normally emphasize what they do well and what they need to work on to get the *design* of the presentation right.

Once the design is right, many of the nervous mannerisms and excessive "uh's" tend to disappear—they're often the product of not knowing what to say next. A good design often takes care of that problem.

At some point, though, you need to say what needs to be said—the problems with delivery that just aren't going away. Most people genuinely appreciate finding out. Usually no one has told them before, and they're relieved to know exactly what to work on. However, I'm careful not to point out any problems the speaker can't change—such as an unusual sounding voice.

You can also give feedback to people after their actual presentation. The best kind is positive if that's at all appropriate. Positive feedback can create a good cycle: people who have succeeded in a presentation gain confidence, and that helps them do better the next time.

Bring up the negatives much later when you're helping the person prepare the next presentation. Even then, I try to stay positive. For example, I don't normally say, "Last time you really screwed up the question-and-answer session because you weren't prepared." Instead, I'd suggest working with that person to prepare the question-and-answer session.

This sounds awfully gentle for a professional situation, but a lack of confidence is a crucial reason most presentations aren't as successful as they should be. Improve the confidence, and the speaking usually improves along with it.

Finally, one of the best ways to help other speakers is to have them help you prepare your presentation. That way they can see the full process for designing a good presentation. And they can see the value of rehearsing.

There are also a couple of suggestions for helping *you* speak better. Look carefully at other speakers and try to understand why their presentation is successful or just ho-hum:

- If you notice someone really effective, ask yourself why. Perhaps there's something special—humor or audience participation or energy—that you'll want to emulate.

- And if you start to get sleepy during a presentation, try to figure out why. What's the speaker doing wrong that's causing you to lose attention?

In effect, you can continue to improve just sitting in the audience—and appreciate what makes most presentations work: an excellent *design!*

Throughout this book, you've seen that plain English aims at keeping ideas clear for members of your audience, whether they are listeners or readers. At the same time, plain English is easier on you, too, whether you're a speaker or a writer.

Many years ago, I dreaded writing and speaking—then plain English revolutionized the way I communicate. I hope it does the same for you!

APPENDIXES

Simpler words and phrases

Bureaucratic	Better
accompany	go with
accomplish	do
advise	tell, recommend
afford an opportunity	let
anticipate	expect
approximately	about
ascertain	find out
assist	help
at the present time	now
attached herewith is	here's
benefit	help
close proximity	near
commence	begin
complete	fill out
conclude	end
concur	agree
cooperate	help
deem	think
demonstrate	show, prove
desire	want
determine	find out
disclose	show
effect	make
elect	choose
endeavor	try

Bureaucratic	Better
ensue	follow
exhibit	show
experience	have
facilitate	help
failed to	didn't
forward	send
furnish	send
furthermore	also
has the capability	can
however	but
identical	same
implement	carry out, do
in addition	also
in an effort to	to
in lieu of	instead of
in the event that	if
in the near future	soon
inasmuch as	since
inception	start
incumbent upon	must
indicate	show
initial	first
initiate	start
insufficient	not enough
legislation	law
limited number	few
locate	find
location	place
maintain	keep, support
modify	change
monitor	check, watch
notify	let someone know
numerous	many, most
observe	see

Bureaucratic	**Better**
permit	let
personnel	people
presently	now
prior to	before
provided that	if
purchase	buy
relating to	about, on
request	ask
require	need
residence	home
retain	keep
reveal	show
review	check, go over
state	say
submit	send
subsequent	later, next
sufficient	enough
supply	send
terminate	stop
therefore	so
this office	we, us
time period	time
transmit	send
transpire	happen
until such time as	until
utilization	use
utilize	use
viable	workable
whereas	since
witnessed	saw

Checklist for speakers

Organization

- Do you clearly announce your topic?

- Do you define key terms in your topic?

- Do you state your bottom line up front (unless your presentation is purely informative)?

- Do you give a blueprint (actual or implied) in your introduction?

- Do you have *strong* transitions beginning each major topic?

Content

- Do you use frequent examples?

Visual aids

- Are your visual aids designed well (uncluttered, read-able, short items rather than long paragraphs)?

- Do you reveal them at the right time—just when the audience needs to turn attention to them?

- Are they visible to everyone in the room (you don't block the screen)?

- Are they straight (for transparencies)?

- Do you use a pointer?

Voice

- Is your speaking free of distractions ("uh," "um," "you know")?

- Do you use natural pauses for emphasis?

- Do you use appropriate loudness: not too soft or too loud?

- Do you use appropriate pace: not too slow or too fast?

Movement

- Do you have *any* purposeful movement around the room?

- Is your movement natural and free of distractions (rocking, pacing, hands in pockets, etc.)?

- Do you use natural hand gestures?

Overall

- Is your audience paying attention at all times?

- Does your audience appear to understand everything you say?

- Do you appear interested in your topic?

- Do you have good eye contact?

- Do you appear obviously rehearsed?

Checklist for setting up the room

Projector and screen

- Does the projector focus well?

- Is there a spare bulb?

- When the transparency is straight on the face of the projector, does it project straight on the screen?

- Is the projected image large enough for the audience to see?

- Is the extension cord from the projector a hazard?

- Is the overhead projector on a table large enough to hold the stack of transparencies you *will* use and the stack you *have* used?

Table and chairs

- Can the audience see the screen clearly from all seats?

- Can you move about freely ?

Microphone

- Do you have a wireless microphone?

- Does it have a new battery?

- Is the volume adjusted correctly?

- Can you turn your head toward the screen and still project clearly?

- Does the microphone have a fastener that works?
- Have you removed badges, necklaces, etc., that can clank against the microphone?

Lighting

- Is the area above the screen unlighted?
- Is the rest of the room at nearly normal lighting?

Temperature

- Is the room slightly on the cool side—especially before the audience has entered the room?
- Do you know where the thermostat is and whether or not you can make adjustments to it?

Outside distractions

- Can you hear any unwanted noises (such as piped-in music)?

Index